Advance Praise for *Dating God*

"...invites readers into genuine, loving, and costly relationship with God. This is a gift for the whole Church."

—Jamie Arpin-Ricci, C.J., author, *The Cost of Community: Jesus, St. Francis & Life in the Kingdom*

"...a fresh new voice in Christian spirituality who reminds us that the Creator is active in every moment of our lives and shows how our lives are filled with, as the Franciscans say, *pax et bonum:* peace and goodness."

—James Martin, S.J., author, *The Jesuit Guide to (Almost) Everything*

"...explores how to maintain a loving, lifelong relationship with God, other human beings, and all creatures—a relationship that begins with taking the time to go on a date with God."

—Murray Bodo, O.F.M., author, *Francis: The Journey and the Dream*

"Spirituality doesn't get any better than this! A splendid book!"

—Michael Leach, author, *Why Stay Catholic? Unexpected Answers to a Life-Changing Question*

"...clear, concise and insightful. *Dating God* is a rich treasure of Franciscan spirituality for a world in need."

—Ilia Delio, O.S.F., author, *Compassion: Living in the Spirit of St. Francis*

"The idea of 'dating God' may be a little jarring at first, but in Brother Daniel P. Horan's hands it becomes an inspired way to find and channel our longing for God. He has done a remarkable job of bringing the wisdom of St. Francis into the Facebook age."

—Paul Moses, author *The Saint and the Sultan*

"I recommend the book for Catholics young and old, but particularly for young adult Catholics in search of a deeper relationship with God."

—Melissa A. Cidade, Center for Applied Research in the Apostolate

"Younger adults particularly will identify with the questions that Horan proposes, happy to discover that the Franciscan tradition can serve as a challenging and responsible guide."

—Fr. Kevin J. Mullen, O.F.M., PH.D., president, Siena College

DATING GOD
Live and Love in the Way of St. Francis

Daniel P. Horan, O.F.M.

franciscan
media
Cincinnati, Ohio

Permission to publish excerpts from *Francis of Assisi: Early Documents* granted by New City Press, New York.

Scripture passages have been taken from *New Revised Standard Version Bible,* copyright ©1989, Division of Christian Education of the National Council of the Churches of Christ in the United States of America. Used by permission. All rights reserved.

"Dating God: A Young Friar's Experience of Solitude" by Daniel P. Horan. Reprinted from *America* with permission of America Press, Inc., © 2007. All rights reserved.

Cover and book design by Mark Sullivan

Library of Congress Cataloging-in-Publication Data
Horan, Daniel P.
Dating God : live and love in the way of St. Francis/ Daniel P. Horan.
p. cm.
Includes bibliographical references (p.   ) and index.
ISBN 978-1-61636-136-5 (alk. paper)
1. Francis, of Assisi, Saint, 1182-1226. 2. Spiritual life—Catholic Church. I. Title.
BX4700.F6H585 2012
248.4'82—dc23
                        2011042891

ISBN 978-1-61636-136-5
Copyright © 2012, by Daniel P. Horan, o.f.m. All rights reserved.

Published by Franciscan Media
28 W. Liberty St.
Cincinnati, OH 45202
www.FranciscanMedia.org

For
Ryan J. Horan
and
Vincent J. Kneller

May you continue to see God in the world and come to realize the Christian vocation you have received on the day of your baptism, which I was so privileged to witness and sponsor as your godfather.

contents

✳

acknowledgments

✳

In any given book, after the index and the list of works cited, the acknowledgements page is the next thing I read before beginning to read the book itself. There is something deeply touching in reading about those people an author wishes to thank and for what reason. Like all books, this one was not written in a vacuum. Many people contributed to conditions that made this text possible.

Most of this book was written during the 2010–2011 academic year while I was teaching in the department of religious studies at Siena College near Albany, New York. I am grateful for the fraternal support and inspiration of my brother friars and for the spirit of collegiality and welcome offered by my faculty colleagues. I am especially thankful for the opportunity to teach such outstanding undergraduate students. Two particular friars deserve appreciative recognition: Brian Belanger, O.F.M., my local guardian, recognized the importance of this project early on and encouraged me to consider it a priority alongside my other academic responsibilities, and Daniel Nelson, O.F.M., who is the caretaker of the friars' Lake George cabin, created an inviting and hospitable environment for my occasional escape from the college campus to work on this manuscript and other projects in the Adirondack Mountains.

I am indebted to Kelly Zientek-Baker, who first encouraged me to publish the manuscript that became the article "Dating God: A Young Friar's Experience of Solitude," which appeared in *America* magazine in June 2007 and from which the title of this book comes. Portions of chapter 4 first appeared in that *America* article.

I owe Hugh Macsherry, O.F.M., and the "20s/30s Boston" young-adult group thanks for inviting me to direct their annual retreat, which was based largely on initial versions of the first chapters of this book, at Glastonbury Abbey in Hingham, Massachusetts, in November 2010. Their interest, questions, discussion, and feedback helped shape some of my earliest drafting of the manuscript. I am also grateful for the invitation to lecture at the Newman Center of Buffalo State College in February 2011, during which time I also presented some material-in-progress for this book and received a gracious welcome.

Julianne Wallace, a dear friend and passionate campus minister at the University at Buffalo, read the earliest drafts of this book and offered helpful feedback and insight. I appreciate her kind, yet direct, comments as the project developed, which strengthened the text while allowing me to connect more effectively with readers. I am thankful for the support of my family, my brother friars, and my friends, especially Andrew and Sarah Kneller, David Golemboski, Brianna Copley, and so many others who are always there to encourage and challenge me.

Finally, I am indebted to the editorial and marketing staff at St. Anthony Messenger Press. Lisa Biedenbach, a fellow St. Bonaventure University alum, deserves countless thanks for her enthusiasm for my work and for her encouragement. Lisa is also responsible for drafting the reflection questions at the end of each chapter. I am also grateful for the professional, patient, and understanding assistance of Mary Carol Kendzia, Mary Curran Hackett, and everyone at SAMP who helped bring this text to completion.

This book is dedicated to my youngest brother and my best friends' oldest son, both of whom I am honored to call my godsons.

Daniel P. Horan, O.F.M.
October 4, 2011
Solemnity of St. Francis of Assisi

introduction

�֎

PRAYER AND RELATIONSHIP

Look at the humility of God,
and *pour out your hearts before him*!
Humble yourselves
that you may be exalted by Him!
Hold back nothing of yourselves for yourselves,
that He Who gives Himself totally to you
may receive you totally!
—Francis of Assisi[1]

A New Way to Understand One's Relationship with God
What does that sound like to you?

These are the words that launched this book several years ago. I was sitting on a very uncomfortable chair in a large room with twenty or thirty other Franciscans during the dead of winter. Twice a year all the Franciscan novices, those men and women in the earliest stages of religious life, gathered together for a weeklong workshop in a large, old retreat center built by the Friars of the Atonement in the middle of the twentieth century (during the boom years for priests and religious). It was originally the site of a seminary but now hosted various retreats in its cavernous facility. I was there with my young Franciscan colleagues for our first experience of this program.

1

During this winter workshop we were treated to the wise and insightful reflections of both a Franciscan friar and a Franciscan sister. This team was an excellent combination. They worked well together and helped open up discussions while sharing the Franciscan tradition better than most of the retreat leaders and workshop presenters I would subsequently experience (and believe me, Franciscan friars and sisters attend many such retreats and workshops).

On one particular afternoon we were given a handout with several selections to read aloud from the writings of both Francis and Clare of Assisi. The passages contained letters from Francis and Clare to their brothers and sisters in faith, some to the friars who had given up their previous lives to follow Francis's model of gospel life and some from Clare to her cousin, Agnes of Prague. All of the texts expressed the attempts of the two saints to articulate what it was that they were experiencing in their relationships with God.

Those of us attending the workshop, new in our own journeys following in the footprints of Francis and Clare, were then asked to reflect on what we read and heard. *What does that sound like to you?* Those present began to share what the writings of Francis and Clare sounded like to them. Some heard the voices of prophets and passages from Scripture, while others recognized in the tone of the texts the desire for God. Still others heard in the honest and endearing reflections of the saints from Assisi echoes of their own experience.

Normally one of the first to talk, I, a rather easily identifiable extrovert, found myself quiet (for once). Something about the medieval writing spoke to my heart in a new, although familiar, way. I could relate to the sharing that was going on around me. Certainly in the words of Francis and Clare there were echoes of Scripture and a strong desire for God and my own experience reflected. But what did it *sound like* to me?

One image kept coming to mind: *dating.* The tone, the desire, the echoes of Scripture, the uncertainty, the love—it all sounded a lot like Francis and Clare understood and even described their relationships with God as one might understand and describe his or her experience of getting to know another person through the process of what we today call "dating." It seemed all too weird. Perhaps that's why I was quieter than usual, but I couldn't shake this idea and I had to share it.

So I did.

What I first shared that afternoon never left me. The idea that one might understand and even describe a relationship with God to be like dating, as bizarre as it first sounds, remained with me as I continued to read the sources in the Franciscan tradition and better come to understand my vocation and my own relationship with God. What I initially shared in its most nascent form, that inkling of inspiration that arose from the writings of Francis and Clare, is what I have sought to share with you in this book.

I hope that this book helps you to consider how God is active and present in your life, while also renewing the way you think about your relationship with God. Drawing on the Franciscan tradition, you might see the gift of Franciscan spirituality anew. In considering your relationship with God to be like dating, you might be able to see life today through the lenses of Francis, Clare, and those who followed in their footprints over the centuries. It will challenge you to reexamine your concept of spirituality, prayer, and relationships, and it will invite you into a more intimate and authentic relationship with your Creator.

Spirituality Is Learning to Love God
Over the course of the last eight hundred years, many in each generation of every new age have looked to Francis and Clare of Assisi, and those who followed them, for spiritual wisdom and guidance. Their

way of life, the *vita evangelica*, or gospel living, is both challenging and assuring, both difficult and easy, both ancient and ever new.

To follow the "gospel of our Lord Jesus Christ," which is what we might describe as Francis's sort of "game plan" in the first chapter of his Rule, requires a certain commitment from each of us. Fundamentally, this commitment is our full acceptance of our baptismal relationship. In baptism each of us was united to Christ and one another in a unique matrix of relationships that, whether we like it or not, bind us together as a community of believers that shares in the saving act of God's love made manifest in the life, death, and resurrection of the Son.

In recent years, some Franciscan scholars, such as Capuchin Franciscan Fr. Regis Armstrong, have taught that Francis in the beginning of his ministry was not interested in founding a religious order but was concerned simply with following his baptismal call in the most authentic manner he could.[2] It was his human vocation, the intrinsic capacity for God deep within each human heart, that he lived to the fullest, and it was this way of living that drew the first brothers and sisters of the newly emerging Franciscan family to seek him for guidance and direction.

One lesson that emerges from the formation of the Franciscan movement is the universal nature of God's call for all to take seriously the challenge of living the gospel. Another lesson that arises from the early Franciscan movement is the communal nature of gospel life. While Francis may have desired only to live out his baptismal commitment in humility, simplicity, and prayer, he quickly discovered that such a life could be lived only in community. To be a Christian does not mean to be in relationship with God *alone* but to live in loving relationship with others. In other words, to be a Christian means embracing the joys and the challenges of being a member of the Body of Christ.

The heart of gospel life is relationship. Therefore, the centerpiece of Franciscan life is relationship. One reason that I believe the Franciscan tradition has lasted so long as a source of spiritual inspiration is the universal appeal it affords people. The gospel message of *relationality*, modeled after God's own example through the Incarnation, is embodied in the way Francis and Clare lived their baptismal commitments. And this shines through in their writings and heritage. Their example continues to offer a source of reflection and a directive path for us today.

Although the times have significantly changed from thirteenth-century Europe to a technologically saturated, increasingly globalized and unavoidably pluralistic world, the human condition remains strikingly unchanged. Our human brokenness and sin continues to affect our outlook and daily encounters, but that intrinsic capacity to desire and know God also remains.

The primary question that guides this book is *How can I know and love God today?* This question will serve as our starting point on a journey toward God. This book is a reflection on how to relate to God and one another in our contemporary setting. It is not an answer book or a schema providing easy steps to or instructions for an ideal prayer life. Rather, it offers a new look at the timeless condition of human longing for a deeper relationship with the Creator. I suggest that the experience of dating provides us with a helpful image to explore Christian spirituality through a fresh lens. Replete with emotional ups and downs, euphoric highs and depressing lows, energy, affection, and fear, our everyday experiences of getting to know another in an increasingly intimate manner might help us to envision our relationship with God in a new and ever deepening way.

The Franciscan tradition is perhaps the best model for this deepening relational experience with the Divine. A close look at the written

Franciscan sources reveals a deeply relational quality of prayer. At times the prayers, letters, and admonitions of Francis and Clare read like poetic depictions of an emerging relationship with a lover. At other times the texts help point the reader to new and unexpected places, only to allow the reader to arrive more closely to God. Spirituality is indeed a journey and, like dating someone, can be filled with wonderful surprises and unforeseen heartache.

Prayer as Relationship

So often prayer is depicted as something we *do*. As an action it loses a sense of incompleteness or development that reflects a more dynamic understanding of what communication with one's Creator entails. Communication as an ongoing and open experience of our whole lives is something that I came to appreciate after witnessing it as something that held people together in love. It was only by experiencing that way of living with others that I came to see how much prayer is more than just something that is said or done.

I was in my early twenties when I entered religious life as a Franciscan friar. Coming to this particular way of living in the world right out of college made me, in some sense, different from a lot of my peers and friends. They went into the workforce or graduate school, some found new boyfriends or girlfriends, and others settled into lifelong commitments with a spouse in marriage and began a new family. My best friend, my college roommate for all four years, married another close friend of mine not too long after we graduated from college. Their relationship is something to be admired for many reasons. Rarely do young adults (or even not-so-young adults) manifest as well as in the shared life of my two friends the mutual self-gift of love about which the Catholic tradition speaks so eloquently. When pressed to reveal what it is about their relationship that so empirically exhibits the love that is otherwise so difficult to express, they offer a simple response: *communication*. It is likely unsurprising that communication is a cornerstone of a healthy relationship, but I suggest that communication for my friends has less to do with a series of regular verbal exchanges than it does with an openness to the other and a mutual attentiveness to the needs, desires, fears, anxieties, joys, and sadness of the one loved.

Communication is a lot more than words. And if prayer is communication with God, then it must be more than the act of speaking (or thinking). We communicate with those we love, with those we are in relationship with, in a variety of ways. Through both verbal and non-verbal communication we make our needs known but also express an attentiveness to the other in solidarity, sympathy, and compassion, or in distance, disinterest, and contempt. One need not speak these things to communicate them to another. What I and others have observed in the case of my two friends is that even when neither says a word, an environment of love and support is somehow made present in their midst. There is nothing particularly magical about this. Instead, it is the expression of the heart made present in their lives.

I would suggest that this type of communication is what we need to consider in our reflection on spirituality. Just as our interpersonal relationships—whether they be with family, friends, or lovers—require us to communicate our whole selves beyond mere words, so too our relationship with God requires us to communicate our whole selves to our Creator. In this sense, my relationship with God becomes a prayer. My relationship with God becomes a total communication that transcends simply verbal expression to include my whole self. This means that my relationship with God *is* my prayer. It becomes an ongoing expression of who I am—with all of my joy and success, all of my pain and sorrow—to God. To view prayer as relationship in light of such a total communication suggests a degree of intimacy that rises above many of our previous experiences of another.

Franciscan theologian Ilia Delio offers a helpful image to illustrate this intimacy. Drawing on the Hebrew understanding of God's Spirit as breath (*Ruach Elohim*), the same breath that the book of Genesis tells us God breathed into the nostrils of the first human beings to give them life (Genesis 2:7), Delio writes: "Prayer is God's desire to breathe in me, to be the Spirit of my life and to draw me into the fullness of life. When I pray, when I breathe with God, I become part of the intimacy of God's life."[3] The intimacy of sharing breath, of breathing together, is reminiscent of the mouth-to-mouth emergency resuscitation that is part of CPR treatment. There is nothing more intimate, nothing more evocative of life and self-gift than to breathe for and with another.

Prayer as relationship suggests a dynamic mutual self-gift between an already present and loving God and the return of such love in a total free-offering of self. This relationship includes verbal and direct expression but is not limited to it. This relationship requires time set apart and dedicated solely for working on this relationship in prayer but remains more than our time in church or private prayer. This relationship has the potential to turn our whole life into a living prayer.

Self-offering is essential to this life of prayer. The Franciscan poet and writer Murray Bodo has written on how this necessary disposition is so often absent in our lives: "Unfortunately, the gestures our lives make tend to be circular and narcissistic, so that it takes real effort to break out of the circle of self, to cross over the dirt road, and ascend or descend into some place of remembering who we really are."[4] What makes the relationship of my friends from college so awe-inspiring is that they work at breaking out of that circle of self-centeredness to remember who they really are. It is only then, recalling their insertion into relationship with God and others, that they are able to work toward full communication and a life transformed, if imperfectly as of yet, into prayer.

Francis and Clare also broke out of that circle of self in order to step more deeply into full communication with God. Perhaps this is what Francis meant when on his deathbed he wrote:

> The Lord gave me, Brother Francis, thus to begin doing penance in this way: for when I was in sin, it seemed too bitter for me to see lepers. And the Lord Himself led me among them and *I showed mercy* to them. And when I left them, what had seemed bitter to me was turned into sweetness of soul and body. And afterwards I delayed a little and left the world.[5]

To leave the world is to leave a false sense of independence, of disinterest in others, of abandonment of God. We see that to move beyond the static and limited understanding of prayer requires us to reimagine our relationship with God. This is what Francis and Clare did nearly eight centuries ago. It is why their lives shine as examples for people of every age and continue to capture the attention and imagination of so many. The life of the Franciscan is to live the gospel, to transform one's entire life into prayer.

Dating God

My feet are planted quite firmly in two worlds. One foot stands in a globalized, technological, and fast-paced world. Born in the early 1980s, I am rather expectantly a child of my generation and comfortable in a digital world. The other foot, clad in the iconic sandal, rests in the displaced dirt that marks the footprint of Francis of Assisi. Having completed my undergraduate education at a Franciscan university, I responded to what I felt deep within was an invitation to walk on a particular journey in this life. I entered the Order of Friars Minor and, for several years, remained the youngest Franciscan friar in my province, the largest group of Franciscan friars in North America. I am a Millennial Franciscan. I share this because this is my starting point. This is, in part, who I am. I wrote this book to offer a new perspective on prayer in light of the Franciscan tradition, with the hope that my experiences might be helpful for all who seek the Divine today, the young and the young at heart alike.

This book is not of the self-help or relationship-advice variety, at least not in the traditional sense. It is a series of reflections on the meaning of prayer and relationship for those who seek God today. Following in the footprints of Francis and Clare of Assisi, as well as those wisdom figures of the tradition that followed them, I will explore what it means to live as a spiritual person today striving toward a deeper relationship with God—and I hope you'll join me.

Some of you, however, might be wondering: *What does a Franciscan friar know about dating?* A fair question. While officially "off the market" now, I once had my fair share of relationships in high school and college. Enough to know the ins and outs of dating and relationships—the high of first falling in love and the low of falling out of love. I know what it is like to break a heart and I have also experienced the pain of heartbreak. I know what the in-between time is like—the fun, bliss, and joy of the early stages and planning as well as the jealousy, fights, and misunderstandings that usually mark the end. And although my time of dating has come to an end, I haven't forgotten the experiences or the feelings. For the sake of my past loves I have been extraordinarily careful to protect their identities here. The lessons I have learned from these varied experiences help shape my own understanding of what it means to give, communicate, and love. The tales that captured my own experiences have been presented in this book in as general a way as possible, for it is not "dating" as such that concerns us here, but rather it is the metaphor or image of dating that serves as a symbol for our relationship with God, a relationship marked by a life lived as prayer.

God is not our boyfriend or girlfriend, nor is God our spouse. Those who like to say that women and men in vowed religious life (like myself) are "married to God" typically take an image of commitment and vocation far beyond its usefulness. It is my hope that we do not subject the image of dating to a similar misrepresentation. Instead, keep in mind that "dating" is an action, a verb, and "spouse" is a status, or noun. To "date God" is to take a particular stance or position toward another. Dating is a way of doing or being. It also evokes a process or ongoing experience that, while at times it may distinguish one's status, more often than not describes one's desire to explore another's truest self. If you take the romantic connotations away from the term *dating*, then you are left with a word that can be applied to any experience of getting to know another.

Think of your best friend. If your experience is like mine, then when you first meet someone who is bound to be a close friend, you are initially very interested in that person. You want to spend lots of time with him or her, getting to know that person's favorite music, food, TV shows, and so on. Perhaps you talk on the phone late into the night or text each other a hundred times a day, updating your new friend on all the useless trivia of your day-to-day life. You might find yourself interested in new things—sports, foods, activities, hobbies that you never tried before. Maybe you stop eating meat because your friend is a vegetarian. Maybe you start going to church because your friend finds it important. Maybe you never wear dress clothes again because your friend has a weird political aversion to the pretense of a suit and tie.

We slowly, or perhaps at times more quickly, find ourselves becoming more like our friend, precisely because we like our friend. And this is an experience that those who are dating also share, but on a much more intimate level. If these things are true of friends and lovers, how much more so should they be true of God?

Mystics through the centuries have described their passionate and intense experiences of God in prayer as though God were a lover. Others, such as the medieval English abbot Aelred of Rievaulx, have considered God as like a friend. Still others, including Jesus of Nazareth, speak of God as a father or a mother. Just as each of these images—lover, friend, and parent—does not exhaust the richness of God's ability to relate to us in ever increasingly personal ways, to think of God in terms of dating will also inevitably fall short of perfection. Nevertheless, I believe that this way of looking at our relationship with God, new as it may seem to us, might be just what today's spiritual seekers need to rekindle a sense of the divine in their lives or to discover it for the first time. An experience like dating that is, a relationship of increasing intimacy, complication, and change—is exactly what Francis and Clare of Assisi knew in their lives lived as prayer. Perhaps it's time that, following their cues, we go on a date with God.

Important Points to Remember

- In addition to the many ways one can envision his or her relationship with God (as friend, parent, lover, and so on), dating provides a new and relevant way to look at prayer and spirituality in a Franciscan tone.
- To be Franciscan is to live out one's baptismal vocation in the world by keeping the gospel central and prioritizing relationship with God and others above all else.

• This book is a reflection on how to relate to God and one another in our contemporary setting. While not an answer book, it does offer a new look at the timeless condition of human longing for a deeper relationship with the Creator and points a way, in the spirit of Francis and Clare of Assisi, toward that experience of the Divine. Prayer is more than just something we do. It is a dynamic experience of communication of our whole lives to God.

Reflection Questions

1. How do I describe my current relationship with God? How has that relationship changed since my childhood?
2. In what ways is God active and present in my life?
3. "To be a Christian does not mean to be in relationship with God *alone* but to live in loving relationship with others" (p. 4). With whom do I live in loving relationship?

chapter one

The First Date
The Pilgrimage Begins

Before I formed you in the womb I knew you,
and before you were born I consecrated you.
—Jeremiah 1:5

Setting Out on the Journey

"Mr. Dan, why are you wearing a brown dress?"

This was the way I was greeted by my friends' four-year-old daughter Alyssa when I arrived at church on the occasion of her older brother's First Communion. Her parents and I, among others, had spoken to her many times before about how "Mr. Dan" (I) was a Franciscan friar and what that meant. However, it is definitely a whole new experience to see a twenty-six-year-old man wearing a religious habit that hasn't been in style for eight hundred years.

Over the years, the kids often asked about what I did for work or why I wasn't married (or looking to be married). No matter how often I explained that I was a friar and what that meant, I was always "Mr. Dan," a friend of the family (and an easy target to be beaten in a game of Wii Bowling or Guitar Hero). The significance of being a Franciscan friar was lost on the little ones. Nevertheless, the question Alyssa asked me that morning has stayed with me because it struck me as more profound than it at first seemed.

While I was certainly not wearing a dress, at least not a dress in a sense that any modern person might be inclined to wear one for an evening on the town, I was in fact publicly expressing something externally that reflected a deep commitment and significant part of who I am internally. The Franciscan habit has, for nearly eight centuries, identified those who have chosen to respond to God's invitation to live the gospel in a unique way following the example of St. Francis of Assisi. It's usually seen in medieval paintings or modern birdbaths depicting the saint from Assisi as "the lover of all creation." It's instantly recognizable.

Although I seriously doubt my young inquisitor knew all that was implied in her observation, I have since been left to grapple with that question: *Why am I a Franciscan friar?* That question, hidden beneath the curiosity that my medieval fashion sense evokes in kids (children *often* ask me if I am a Jedi knight or Luke Skywalker from *Star Wars*), is really a question about my personal journey.

How is it that I came to wear this "brown dress?"

I never wanted to be a Franciscan friar. But then again we usually don't know what we want—at least not at first. It would be a series of events, recognizable only after the fact, on my life journey that would direct and redirect the formation of my becoming who I am. Each of us is, whether we choose to acknowledge it or not, on a journey of becoming who God calls us to be.

Such was the case with a young man in the Umbrian region of Italy in the early thirteenth century. Francis of Assisi didn't start his life as the saint we remember him to be today. While some of his biographers, like St. Bonaventure of Bagnoregio, describe him as a generous, loving, and all-around good guy from the beginning, other authors, like Thomas of Celano, depict Francis as being less than holy at the start. We can assume that Thomas of Celano, who wrote his *Life of Saint*

Francis within three years of the saint's death, exaggerated the severity of Francis's sinful behavior to emphasize his conversion. A lot of people who are a little familiar with Francis's story have the Thomas of Celano impression of the young saint's character. However, my view of Francis is closer to Bonaventure's portrayal of the man. Francis was basically a normal guy who was neither depraved nor predictably a saint.

The earliest sources tend to agree that Francis was a gregarious young man who liked partying with his friends and enjoyed the comfortable lifestyle afforded by his father's success as a cloth merchant. He was busy with the concerns of his time and the activities that any "middle-class" young adult of his era would be interested in. One might imagine Francis as someone like the average college student in the United States today. Most young adults are not malicious or "sinful" in their own right, but they are not often concerned with issues that reach beyond their particularly limited world of friends, classes, parties, and so on.

The young Francis was similarly limited in his outlook, concerned most with impressing his peers, having a good time, helping out around his father's business, and dreaming about becoming an honorable knight (this was the Middle Ages, remember). It is fair to say that Francis was not at all interested in becoming a friar or a penitential mendicant. He was not thinking about founding a religious community that would grow to be the largest order in the Church, and he was certainly not aware of where God was eventually going to invite him to journey in life. He went from being a normal and otherwise indistinguishable young man of his age to become one of the most popular Christian saints of all history—all because of his increasingly intense relationship with God.

Like Francis of Assisi, each of us journeys along the pilgrimage of life, and while doing so we are being shaped in little unseen ways. Only occasionally do we become aware of the liminal moments that change our lives forever in large and significant ways. One of the insights Francis's story provides for us today is that, although we begin our part of the journey in varied times and ways, God has always been there alongside us from the beginning. For many of us, it is only when we stop and look back on our lives that we can see where the Spirit was indeed breaking into our world. Spirituality is in large part a matter of becoming ever more attentive to the questions and subsequent answers of our lives. *Who am I? Where did I come from? Where am I going?*

When I was a young child attending Our Lady of Lourdes elementary school in Utica, New York, I could not wait to be an altar server. My family was not extraordinarily religious but was committed nonetheless to going to Mass every weekend. Because of both the Christian environment of the elementary school I attended and my parents' insistence that we go to Mass as a family each week, I knew instinctively that church was important. This backdrop of faith set the stage where I would come to develop a strong desire to be involved at church. During a time when only boys were allowed to put on the cassock and surplice, becoming an altar boy captured my attention like nothing else. I was enraptured by the thought of being near what was happening in the sanctuary and being able to do the special duties the priests entrusted to the other altar boys.

It was not until fifth grade that I finally got the chance to be an altar server. It was awesome. The altar boys used to be assigned for a week at a time to serve the early morning Mass at 6:30. We newbies would be paired up with an older, more experienced server to learn the ropes. Kevin, a boy a year or two older than I, was the one tasked with showing me all that I needed to know. I absorbed it all like a sponge. I loved every minute of being an altar server. I would later go on to work as the sacristan for my home parish while in high school and, although my interests changed from one thing to the next during those teenage years, the Church and the liturgy always held a special place in my life.

When I look back on my short life, I think it's fair to say that my pilgrimage to becoming a Franciscan friar, my journey to eventually wearing that "brown dress," began that first week as an altar server. What is important to realize is that, while I was drawn to service in the Church, it wasn't as a Franciscan or member of another kind of religious order (such as the Jesuits, Dominicans, Carmelites, etc.); at that time I simply didn't know what a religious order was. In fact, I didn't *really* know what a Franciscan was until I went to college. All I knew was the diocesan priesthood. I was blessed to have the example of kind and dedicated priests for and with whom I worked. That was what I thought I wanted to be. But that's a story for later. What is important for me to say now is that, as I look back, moments like the first time I woke up before sunrise to serve at Mass represent for me concrete experiences of connecting with the divine. One could say that this was my *first date* with God. For me, such precious moments remind me of my vocation to live out my life as a Christian in a unique and particular way—as "Daniel Horan" and not as someone trying to be somebody else.

We are each on a pilgrimage, a journey toward becoming more and more who we are. There are lots of ways to describe what such a journey looks like and how we might best understand the path of our lives. One way is to talk about vocation. Growing up attending Catholic schools, vocation was for me generally connected to becoming a priest or a nun. But the term *vocation* is much richer and more personal than that definition. I suggest that *vocation* is still too rich to be used in its more common form to refer to "priesthood / religious life," "married life," and "the single life." Instead, I like to use Thomas Merton's understanding of vocation. In his book *No Man Is an Island* he writes:

Each one of us has some kind of vocation. We are all called by God to share in His life and in His Kingdom. Each one of us is called to a special place in the Kingdom. If we find that place we will be happy. If we do not find it, we can never be completely happy. For each one of us, there is only one thing necessary: to fulfill our own destiny, according to God's will, to be what God wants us to be.[1]

To say that each person has a vocation means more than to say that each person can be classified into a particular way of life, career path, or social status. Instead, to say that each person has a vocation is to speak about the very core of who each person is as individually loved and created into existence by God. Francis knew this well. Toward the end of his life he was remembered to have said to his brothers concerning the way they were to live, "I have done what is mine; may Christ teach you what is yours!"[2]

The goal of our pilgrimage of life is ultimately God. But it is also a journey toward becoming who we truly are, or, as Merton said, "to fulfill our own destiny, according to God's will, to be what God wants us to be." To be a spiritual person is to be aware of this connection between who we are in God's eyes and how we live our lives. The decisions we make, the way we interact with others, the way we treat the environment—all of these things flow from who we are in relationship to God. Francis's ongoing discovery of who he was and who he was called to become arose from his relationship to God. My own following in Francis's footprints, wearing the Franciscan habit (or "brown dress"), and living in such a way as to strive (even if, at most times, I do so imperfectly) toward a fuller understanding of who I am and who I am called to become also arises from my relationship to God. This is what is meant by my vocation. This is what is meant by my journey toward God.

The Journey of Relationship

Every relationship begins somewhere. Some begin romantically with our hearts alive in the excitement of getting to know someone who we are drawn to for the very first time. Some begin at our birth with our introduction to our family. Some begin at school or work, where we first meet our peers and colleagues. Some begin at our baptism, when the immersion into water symbolizing both our dying and rising with Christ signifies our inherent immersion into a set of relationships (the entire Body of Christ, which is the Church) that can never be undone. Yet, there is one relationship that begins before all others.

Some relationships are deeply intimate, where we reveal our true selves and are open to the other person's true self, as with a spouse, close sibling, or best friend. Sometimes those same relationships are difficult or strained, causing us to doubt our ability to love and be loved. Sometimes our experience of others becomes stagnant and boring. Apathy takes grip and we become disinterested in another. Some relationships are simply professional, casual, or superficial and nothing more becomes of them. Some relationships will last for a lifetime, while others last for just a short stint. Yet, there is one relationship that will last forever.

Everybody, whether conscious of it or not, has a relationship with God. The fact that you or I exist, or that anybody exists, testifies to the reality that we are in relationship with our Creator. One medieval theologian describes this relationship as that of an artist to her artwork. There is a preexisting relationship between a painting and a painter: The choice to create when one does not need to do so can signal love, the reflection of the particular artist in the image through unique and unrepeatable brushstrokes can point beyond the creation to the creator, and the beauty of the image—even with its inevitable imperfections—brings to mind the truth that there is something wonderful about life. But we are more than paintings and God is more than a painter.

I firmly believe that all human beings, by virtue of simply *being human*, have a capacity for God that is fundamental and part of the deepest core of who we are. I also believe that God is already and always extending an invitation to us to be in relationship. But how do we recognize this presence of God in our lives? If it is true that God is already there for and with us, why is it that I don't see, feel, hear, or know God all the time? I know what it is like to be in relationship with another person, but what does it mean to say that I am in a relationship with God? These are the questions that guide this book. These are the questions that have challenged and inspired generations of people over the course of millennia. These are our questions.

Learning to See the World Around You

The world in which we live shades the way we see one another. For example, unlike people during the early part of the twentieth century and earlier, we have instant access to cultures, geographies, philosophies, and other ways of thinking from all reaches of the globe, thanks to the advent of the Internet. The way we relate to one another through social-networking sites like Facebook or MySpace is another significant shift from the way even my parents' generation related to others. One of the positive aspects of this new form of relating is our ability to connect with others and be aware of, as *Gaudium et Spes* points out, the "joys and hopes, the griefs and anxieties" of men and women we might never meet.[3] This awareness unites us as a global family that helps us to move beyond the limits of our individual lives. No longer are we limited, even in the most remote town in the most rural part of the country, to our own parochial experiences (unless, of course, we choose to limit ourselves). The Internet, satellite or cable TV, and cell phones link us to each other in amazing ways. But our modern world also has a way of isolating and separating us from one another.

A friend of mine, a theology professor at a large Catholic university, recently told me the story of his encounter with the isolation caused by technology. He had just given a lecture on the challenges to spirituality today. He mentioned that his experience on the same campus over the course of several years led him to believe that the spirit of campus community had grown colder, disconnected, and apathetic in gradual but noticeable ways. He attributed much of this to iPods and cell phones. Before, a decade earlier, he used to walk across campus, greeting and being greeted by others. Today he walked across campus to the deafening silence of zombielike undergrads marching from one building to another to the beat of their personal playlists. The cloud of iPod-induced silence was broken only by an even greater distraction: cell phones. Cell phones seemed to transport the minds of these students to another place, preventing them from seeing what was right in front of their faces. How could a young person on this campus see God if she couldn't even see the other person in front of her face?

Immediately after the class, my friend was walking down the hallway of an academic building when, coming from the opposite direction, one of his students approached while talking on his cell phone. My friend greeted him with a "hello!" But the student did not respond and kept walking straight ahead. The professor, frustrated yet again by this type of experience, followed the student to another building. All the while the student remained oblivious to his professor's presence just a few feet behind him. At one point my friend sped up his stride and, getting ahead of the student, knelt down in the middle of the hallway directly in the path of the oncoming cell-phone user. Just before tripping over his kneeling professor, the student realized there was something in front of him and stopped. But he did not get off the phone. He just stood there, finishing his conversation while his professor looked up from below. Finally, the student hung up the phone and asked the professor, "What are you doing here?" To which my friend replied, "Obviously you didn't listen in class."

Although today's technologies provide us with amazing capacities to connect with others, they can also distract us from seeing the world right around us. In his effort to instantly gratify his desire to talk on the phone, the student my friend encountered was unable to see the living, breathing human being right before him. With the great gifts modern technology give us comes the responsibility to discern when spending time on Facebook or the cell phone or glued to our iPods disconnects us from reality—to discern in order to connect us to a real existence. This is perhaps one of the greatest challenges to developing our relationship with God. Just as we are unable to give our full attention to a friend or spouse when we are typing away on a BlackBerry or browsing the web on an iPhone, so too we realize how difficult it is to "connect" with God in prayer when preoccupied with our gadgets and incessant (and usually unimportant) communication.

I remember one of the saddest restaurant scenes that I have ever witnessed. A few years ago I was out to dinner with a friend near Washington, D.C. She and I were having a great time and enjoying some fantastic food at my favorite restaurant in the area. At a table near us was a middle-aged couple who appeared to be married. About halfway through dinner I found myself gazing over in their direction, suddenly aware that I hadn't heard either of them speaking the whole time my friend and I sat just a few feet away eating and talking. And then I realized why. With heads looking down toward the table, both the man and the woman had a BlackBerry in hand, typing away to

God-knows-whom. Here they were, in *real life*, sitting at a table in a nice restaurant disconnected from each other in order to connect to something else in *virtual life*. They continued to carry on with their texting, e-mailing, web surfing, or whatever they were doing until they left the place. I remember how sad I felt that neither person could bring him- or herself to look up from the phone to see the other person that they were supposed to be in relationship with. What sort of relationship was that?

Technology is not inherently bad or evil, but like all things it needs to be approached with moderation. Like the student in my friend's class and the couple from the restaurant, I know how often I am distracted by hours staring at Facebook or surfing the net or wandering around with iPod buds in my ears, oblivious to the details of the world around me. Part of the Franciscan wisdom that comes to us from the stories of Francis's own conversion is our recognition of the need we all have to learn to see the world around us. Although he didn't have to worry about being distracted with Twitter updates, Francis had his own distractions. It was only over time that he began to see the need to "disconnect" from those distractions in order to see the beauty of God's creation, including the gift that other people were to him in his life.

We can see how much more the need to disconnect from our distractions in order to see the world around us is present today with the omnipresence of technology and entertainment in our modern lives. Even Google's CEO, Eric Schmidt, in his commencement address to the class of 2009 at the University of Pennsylvania, urged the graduates to take a break from the digital world and focus instead on human relationships. An Associated Press reporter summarized the address by saying that Schmidt urged the young people to "find out what is most important to them—by living analog for a while."[4] That the CEO of

Google recognizes the challenge of a life saturated with technology, and the value of disconnecting from it, is a sure sign that we have reached a point of serious concern. The first consequence of technological distraction is likely our interpersonal relationships. Like the couple at the restaurant, we cannot really be present to our loved ones if we are instead present to something else. But furthermore, if we cannot be present to our loved ones whom we can see, how much more absent will God seem to us?

As we reflect on our pilgrimage journeys through life, exploring where it is we've come from, who we are and where we are going, the first step—the first *date*—requires us to make little changes in our lives. We need to learn to be more attentive to the world around us. We need to learn to see the path of our journeys and listen to the ways Christ is teaching us what is ours to do in this life. When our technologies distract us from life, we need to learn to disconnect from them in order to connect to those with whom we are in relationship. We need to learn that God is already always present to us, sitting on the other side of the restaurant table, waiting for us to look up from our worldly distractions and share our life.

Important Points to Remember

- Each of us is on a journey of becoming who we are as called by God, whether we choose to acknowledge it or not. The goal of our journey is ultimately God.
- Francis of Assisi went from being a normal and otherwise indistinguishable young man of his age to become the most popular Christian saint of all history—all because of his increasingly intense relationship with God.

- Spirituality is in large part a matter of becoming ever more attentive to the questions and subsequent answers of our lives—questions such as *Who am I? Where did I come from? Where am I going?*
- We are already always in relationship with God, we just need to learn how to recognize the presence of God in our lives and respond to that invitation God offers us to be in relationship.
- Technology, like many other things in life, can be both helpful and distracting. We need to learn how to see the world around us by focusing on our relationships with one another and God.

Reflection Questions

1. What has been the path of my own spiritual pilgrimage up to this point? What events or moments can I identify now as significantly shaping my experience of self and God? Who do I desire to be? Who does *God desire* me to be?

2. Do I believe that I must start out in life as a saint in order to eventually become the person whom God has called me to be? How is Francis's early experience like or unlike my own?

3. In what ways do I see Christ teaching me what is mine to do in this life?

4. Am I conscious of my relationship or capacity for a relationship with God? What are the ways that I live that reflect that realization? In what ways do I fall short?

5. How do I see the use of modern technology as enabling me to be more fully myself, and how do I see such use as a limiting factor in my life? How can I better learn to see the world around me?

chapter two

What We Are Before God
The True Self

God is the One who is closer to you than you are to yourself.
—St. Bonaventure[1]

Finding the Tree in the Forest

Recently I was driving up to the Lake George area of the Adirondack National Park in New York. Much of this book was written north of the lake, at a small cabin that has been a place of retreat for the Franciscan friars of my province for decades. Over the course of the year during which I taught theology in the department of religious studies at Siena College, I would occasionally go away for a day or two to work on this book and other writing projects. One day while I was driving along the winding roads of the forest lined with beautiful and densely packed trees, I heard on NPR an interview with an author about his new book.

Richard Horan (no relation to me) recently published a book titled *Seeds: One Man's Serendipitous Journey to Find the Trees That Inspired Famous American Writers from Faulkner to Kerouac, Welty to Wharton.* The premise of his book, an adventure across the United States to the birthplaces and former homes of famous American authors, rested on his conviction that there existed trees that inspired the literary creativity of some of the most famous writers of the past two centuries.

Horan's belief wasn't that there were trees in general but that there were particular trees, specific trees under whose shade certain authors took shelter, individual trees whose beauty inspired poetry and prose, singular trees whose history was inextricably intertwined with the most recognized names in print. It wasn't a belief that pine trees or maple trees or rose bushes in general spoke to the creative hearts of these writers. Horan's was a belief that there were actual, individual, unique, and particular trees in real places that affected the lives of these actual, individual, unique, and particular human beings.

As I first listened to the radio host interview Horan, I was skeptical of the value of such an endeavor. But then it began to dawn on me. What Horan was talking about, what he identified from a literary perspective, was something that arose from a truth about reality, a truth that was inherently Franciscan. It was a way of viewing creation and creation's relationship to God in a unique way that recognized the radical contingency and beauty of the created order.

By *contingency* I mean that everything, literally everything that exists, could otherwise not have existed, or could have existed in some other way. Nothing in creation is *necessary*, yet everything in creation is here. Why? And the beauty of creation, that inspirational muse that Horan saw in this or that particular tree and its relationship to this or that particular author, clearly has affected and continues to affect the hearts and minds of men and women of every age. Even as I listened to Horan explain his arbor adventure with the radio host, I saw the beauty of God's love reflected in the creation that surrounded my drive deeper into the mountains.

A Subtle Recommendation

All of this led me to the realization that I think what the world needs are more dunces. Now don't get me wrong. I'm not suggesting that we would be better off with an increasing population of stupid, dense, or clueless people. Nor would I advocate for a society of simpletons or anybody else that you might initially associate with the term *dunce*. On the contrary, I believe that we need more people who fit the original definition of *dunce*: someone who is an intellectual follower of the medieval Franciscan philosopher and theologian John Duns Scotus.

Hear me out. The term *dunce* started out as a something like a compliment that meant one's argument or way of thinking resembled the complex and nuanced thought of Duns Scotus. Our medieval friend and first dunce is also known by his nickname of honor, "the Subtle Doctor," for his arguments are extraordinarily particular and detailed. But over time our term of endearment began to be misused. Some of Duns Scotus's ideas were seen as too radical by later generations, and therefore some considered it an insult to be associated with that name. Others, likely unfamiliar with the actual work of the medieval Franciscan, mistook his association with subtlety for dim-wittedness, and hence the tradition of sitting in the classroom corner and wearing a special cap. When I talk about wanting more dunces, I mean that first definition.

John Duns Scotus had a lot of original ideas. Even those who don't agree with his particular approach to philosophy and theology cannot deny his brilliance. One of those original ideas has to do with what it means to be a person. And not what it means to be a person in general but what it means to be you or me—that is, a particular person. This is a theme that concerned a lot of people in Duns Scotus's time, as it might today. We can look around and see more than six billion human beings living on this planet, and Duns Scotus's question is simple: What makes that person *that* person, and me *me*?

There are lots of ideas that were proposed. One popular explanation stemmed from first identifying something shared in common with others and then looking at the differences. The thing shared in common is called the substance, and the differences made up the form. So, for example, my substance is "human" and the Queen of England's substance is also "human." But, clearly, it's not our substance that makes us who we are. It's the form, which consists of many qualities, such as height, weight, age, color, shape, and so on. I'm a human being (substance), but what makes me *me* are all my accidents (form).

Duns Scotus did not like this setup. One of the things he didn't like was that these qualities of the form keep changing. If what, at least in part, makes me *me* is my weight, how can baby Dan, who weighed seven pounds, be the same person as college Dan, who weighed 150 pounds? Was I a different person? Am I now? I suppose in some ways we are always evolving, maturing, and growing, and yet we are also the *same* person we always were.

Another problem with this view of personhood is that the image of God that emerges and the view of our relationship with God results in some inadequate perspectives (at least from a Franciscan perspective). According to this popular model that Scotus didn't like, the substance or general thing that everybody shares is more important, it comes first. It's sort of like God has a big tub of "human" (think Play-Doh) and kind of molds a Dan, Steve, or Brianna out of it. Who we are is secondary to the idea of some generic human or, more specifically, of "human-ness."

Against this view Duns Scotus presented an alternative perspective. Instead of being concerned first about the what-ness of something ("human-ness"), God was—and we should be—first concerned with the *this*-ness of something. Scotus used the literal Latin term for this and called it *haecceitas* (this-ness). God didn't first love the idea of "human" or my substance and then decide to make a Dan. No, for Duns Scotus, God's plan for my existence centered on me, just as God's plan for bringing you into the world centered on you. God first loved Dan or Steve or Brianna.

This understanding of what makes someone who he or she really is also applies to everything in creation. I bet that Richard Horan would really like John Duns Scotus and his idea of *haecceitas*. Duns Scotus believed that all of creation in each aspect of its individuality bears this thisness, that every blade of grass, every rock, every tree is unique and unreplicable. Duns Scotus would likely have blessed Horan's quest to find this or that particular tree in his effort to identify the inspirational plant because, like Horan, Duns Scotus recognized that uniqueness of all God's creation in its particularity.

The reason I think that the world could use more dunces is because of the way one can start to reimagine or reconsider one's self, others, and all creation from this perspective. Additionally, when we follow Duns Scotus's Franciscan outlook, our view of God also begins to change. Duns Scotus believed that what makes me *me* and you *you* is this principle called *haecceitas*, which is neither exterior nor coincidental to a person (as hair color or height are). Instead, the thing that makes me an individual is identical with my very existence and my humanity. It's about the dignity of particularity. I'm not just some human who happens to be Dan, but I'm Dan who is unique, irreplaceable, unrepeatable, and individually loved by God. And so are you. We all are. This view of what it means to be a particular person centers on God's overabundant generosity and love. We didn't happen by chance or after the fact or as "plan B." No, we each came into existence because God loved us as we are from the beginning.

This perspective brings with it a number of unsettling challenges to those who haven't thought this way before or who see the world more like those who thought substance comes first. One challenge is the appreciation of inherent dignity that comes directly from God. If who we are is identical with our very being, from the first moment of our existence we have a unique value and personhood. Each person's value does not come from the outside, based on what others think (or even from what we think about ourselves). It's not based on who our parents are, what sort of work we do, how much money we have, what we've done or not done, and so on. Our dignity rests at the core of who we are.

This means, of course, that just as we have to value ourselves, to see ourselves as God does, so too do we have to see that unique value and dignity in others. There is no such thing as a human person without dignity or value in the eyes of God, and therefore that should be the case for us too. Even the worst criminal and the most despised person bear this unique *haecceitas* within them. Those whom we find difficult to love are especially challenging to us when we search for all sorts of excuses to hate or dismiss them. But Duns Scotus's view reminds us to see others as God sees them—individually loved into existence. Now this doesn't mean that they will see themselves in this light, just as we so often don't see it in ourselves. This is perhaps one significant cause for such hatred and wrongdoing in our world. We easily forget what it means for us to be created in the image and likeness of God.

You Have to Know Yourself First

Most good relationship advisors and counselors will say that in order to have a healthy relationship with someone else, you have to first have a healthy relationship with yourself. In other words, you have to know yourself before you can really know another person. We all know others' horror stories or have experienced difficult situations ourselves because we didn't follow this advice. Chances are we've all been there and done that before. I know I have.

When I was in college a good friend of mine went about the world in such a way that his closest friends (myself included) were often concerned about what his future held. Not that this guy was in any particular trouble. On the contrary, *particularity* was precisely his trouble. His focus was scattered and fickle, shifting all the time. You might say that he lacked any clear direction. He was a smart, good-looking guy who was fun to be around. But, like so many people, especially young people, the struggle he faced in getting to know himself bled over into trouble with his relationships. This was most clear in his relationships with women. He would date lots of women (not usually at the same time, but it was known to happen) and it would seem that with each change in girlfriend came a significant change in his personality. Now, this wasn't the type of change of habit or preference that comes when we are with someone new, like when I started eating a lot of spaghetti squash and yogurt while dating this woman in college who was really into organic food. What I'm talking about here is that this guy's identity was almost swallowed up by each person he was dating. Nearly everything changed. He was like a convert to each new religion of personality—changing into a completely new person several times a year. What the rest of his friends and I realized was that our pal simply didn't know who he was and so he was constantly looking outside himself to find it. Not surprisingly, he never did find it there.

When we do what my friend did—look outside ourselves to find who we are—our relationships inevitably suffer. We cannot build a strong foundation for a relationship with other people without first knowing ourselves. Without that self knowledge, what can we bring of ourselves to the relationships? It took many years, but my friend did find himself. Years of switching graduate programs, jobs, and girlfriends eventually led him to stop looking outside and to get to know himself. It was only at that point that he was able to finally bring who he is to another person and allow himself to be known while at the same time really get to know his partner for who she is and not just to search for himself. He is married now to a wonderfully gifted woman who can love him for who *he* really is and he can do likewise, as well as love her completely for who she is too.

The wisdom of Duns Scotus provides us with a little map to finding who we are. Just as my friend had to find himself to ultimately find his life partner and a meaningful relationship, we have to find ourselves to find God. Thomas Merton, in his book *New Seeds of Contemplation*, says that where we find God is at the same point that we discover our True Self. Following the same tradition of spirituality present in the Franciscan view of the world, the view found in Duns Scotus's notion of *haecceitas*, Merton develops the concept of thisness in terms of our True Self. The True Self is discernible only within because, as Duns Scotus explained, who we are is, at its core, identical with our very existence. When we look outside of ourselves and try to be something or someone whom God did not create us to be, we build our false self. Merton explains:

> Everyone of us is shadowed by an illusory person: a false self.
>
> This is the man I want myself to be but who cannot exist, because God does not know anything about him....
>
> My false and private self is the one who wants to exist outside the reach of God's will and God's love—outside of reality and outside of life. And such a self cannot help but be an illusion.[2]

The more we try to build up our false self, the less able we are to connect to God and others. We can, like my college friend, become consumed by external images of who we should be or want to be, or even become swallowed up by another person's personality. Merton makes it clear that this false self simply cannot exist, it's an illusion that only serves to distract us from the reality of who we really are, who God really is, and what it means to really be in relationship. How long can a relationship really last when one person is not being entirely honest about who they are? There are dozens of romantic comedies that play on this theme over and over again. We all know what happens. Eventually the false self, the image conjured up by one of the characters, is recognized as such by the love interest—and the relationship can no longer continue. It's not until the character, previously preoccupied by an image that he needed to project, finally discovers himself as he really is that the love interest is then able to begin seeing him as his True Self.

While our human relationships also rely on our ability to own and put forward our True Self, our relationship with God is even more closely tied to that reality. For it is God who created our True Selves, our unique and unrepeatable *haecceitas*, which is why Merton says that God cannot know our false selves—God didn't create them, we did. If we have any hope and desire to know God, to be in relationship with God, we have to first know our True Self.

The True Self and the Digital Self

There are many ways the false self comes to be the focus of our energy. Most often it stems from insecurity about how acceptable we are just as we are. The false self can also be bolstered or emphasized by our culture. One of the biggest sources, both of personal insecurity and emphasis on the false self, comes in the form of social media. We are bombarded with images and messages that constantly tell us that we need to change or become X, Y, or Z. So much of our energy as a society is placed on adjusting to those external demands placed on us to be this way or that way, to be younger, thinner, smarter, or whatever. And there are an infinite number of products and services we can purchase to reach those goals. But they never bring happiness; and they will almost certainly distract us from discovering who we really are, our True Self.

I don't know about you, but I spend way too much time on Facebook. It's a common complaint in my circle of friends: "Join Facebook, waste time!" There are definite advantages to participating in new forms of social networking like Facebook, MySpace, and LinkedIn. But there are clear disadvantages too. I like that I can connect with people I would otherwise lose touch with, share photographs, and comment on the happenings of everyday life. However, I dislike that I often feel sucked into the mundane details of everybody's life (so-and-so is "shopping at the mall, hope there's a sale!"), see far too many inappropriate images from parties and vacations, and get dragged into too many ideological disputes over *New York Times* columns that I or someone else happened to repost online.

What is really concerning, though, from the perspective of spirituality and my relationship with God, is how much of my energy goes toward shaping and reshaping my digital identity. Unlike "real life," in "virtual life" you get to create and project whatever image of yourself that you want. It may be of lesser or greater resemblance to the person of real time and space, but it is almost entirely your creation. I wasn't born with a Facebook page (although perhaps infants will soon have them). I *created* a Facebook page. I *created* an identity, which Merton and Scotus would say falls into the category of the false self. Don't get defensive just yet. Just because it's the false self doesn't mean that it's bad or malicious. What I mean (with Merton and Scotus to back me up) is that we are simply putting our efforts in the wrong place. The natural desire to share myself with others is good, but the answers to the ultimate questions of meaning in this life won't be found in your Facebook newsfeed or on Justin Timberlake's Twitter updates.

I like to say that if Jesus had been born around 1980 and got started with his public ministry around 2010, he might have "friended" the twelve apostles on Facebook but would have sent an "e-vite" to them shortly afterward for an in-person meeting. Technology offers us a variety of great tools, but it's when we lose sight of their utility and start treating them as ends in themselves that we become preoccupied with our Digital Self, a modern version of the false self. To borrow a phrase from Merton (if Merton were alive to have witnessed the dawn of social media), we cannot find God with our Digital Self, nor can God find us, because God does not know the Digital Self.

I'm not a luddite, someone who hates technology, but I do see the limits technology offers us in our quest to be in relationship with God. One of the greatest challenges of our age is the need to disconnect from technology in order to reconnect to ourselves, others, and God. The problem is that so few people see the need to do that. What we need to do is remember to look within to find our true identity and not be so preoccupied with the external pressures or demands to establish who we are beyond or apart from our God-given *haecceitas*, our True Self.

One of St. Francis's most telling bits of wisdom comes to us in one of his twenty-three Admonitions. St. Francis, whose life was the model and inspiration for John Duns Scotus and even Thomas Merton, traveled around to communities of his brother friars in the early thirteenth century. On one such occasion, while speaking to a group of men who had chosen to leave their previous ways of living to follow the gospel according to St. Francis, he said: "What you are before God, that you are and nothing more."[3] St. Francis knew that what we needed to do to see ourselves as we truly are is to look at ourselves with the eyes of God. How does one see that inherent dignity, that unique identity that makes up our True Self? One looks in the mirror of the soul with the eyes of the loving God who created each of us as he or she really is. No more, no less.

St. Francis is talking about what Scotus and Merton would develop further: In order to know God (or anybody else, for that matter), we must first know ourselves. We do not always think especially positively about ourselves. Sometimes we think too negatively, which is just as much a problem. What looking at ourselves as God does provides us with is an honest look at each person as uniquely brought into this world in love. Another medieval Franciscan saint and theologian, Bonaventure, put it this way: "I see myself better in God than in myself."[4] No one is, at the most basic and human level, better or worse than another. Every life is sacred. It is only in embracing that image of ourselves and others that we are able to in turn embrace God.

"A Sister, Spouse, Mother of the Lord"

Like St. Francis, St. Clare of Assisi has an incredibly relational understanding of God. Although we have very few of her original writings, what we do have reveals the deeply intimate perspective of what a life of Christian living should look like. Speaking of Jesus Christ, she often uses the phrase "a sister, spouse, and mother" when advising Agnes of Prague in the spiritual life. It is clear that, for the most part, St. Clare has a very spousal conception of her (and Agnes's) relationship to God. She reflects a lot on the choice to "give up" an earthly spouse in exchange for a heavenly "spouse of more noble stock." But although St. Clare's writing seems a little outdated and not exactly relevant for twenty-first-century Christians, a closer look reveals timely wisdom. And although her letters are directed to another woman in vowed religious life and have a particular style, her understanding of the spiritual life can help us understand ourselves, and therefore God, better.

A theme that comes through strongly in St. Clare's writings is her love of poverty. At first glance it can be hard for contemporary people (particularly middle-class folks in the United States) to feel comfortable talking about poverty, let alone desiring it as a good. However, what St. Clare is talking about is first and foremost a reexamination of what is important in our lives. What is it that we look to in order to find meaning? Each of her letters to Agnes of Prague begins with a joyful praise of Agnes's abandonment of her royal lifestyle and privilege to focus not on this world's rewards but on those of God. See, Agnes was a princess. Yeah, the real deal. She would have, had things gone as planned, married a prince or a duke in Europe and continued to live a privileged, wealthy, and luxurious life. Instead, she left it all to enter a Franciscan monastery (what today we would call a "Poor Clare" community of cloistered women), having given everything up to live a life of prayer. It would be like Prince William of England deciding to renounce his royal status and the throne to enter a Trappist monastery somewhere in England.

In some ways this is an extreme example. It's not every day (especially not today) that the wealthy, the noble, or the powerful give up things of this world so dramatically to live a life of prayer and gospel poverty. But this is why their stories, the story of Agnes, are so important—because they're sort of the extreme version of everybody's life. Most of us simply live more or less comfortable lives. Those who are fortunate might have a job and a home that is not lavish, but neither are we destitute. And although we might never be in a position to renounce the throne of England or an inheritance from Bill Gates or Oprah Winfrey, we do face the same challenge of where to look for our meaning or purpose. Perhaps it's in the gadgets and technology we use: Am I always looking to be the first to have the latest smartphone, iPad, or video-game console? Perhaps it's in money: Do I search for my identity in how large my back account is or in my portfolio's return? Perhaps it's in the clothes I wear, and in religious life in particular this can work the other way—a competition in who has the "poorest" clothing: Do I seek recognition or status for being the nicest- or poorest–attired person? Or, perhaps we, like my friend in college, find our meaning and identity in other people: *Do I determine who I am based on who I think others are?*

St. Clare praises the former princess, Agnes, for giving up all worldly possessions and royal marriage, because it is the most concrete way to abandon the search for meaning in the wrong places. Looking for meaning in things and property? St. Clare says: "Choose poverty!" Looking for meaning in your relationships as sister, spouse, or mother? St. Clare says: "Choose first those relationships with God!" Or, to put it another way, look for who you *really* are in relationship with who God really is. Dating God is just another way of talking about being in relationship with the one who needs nothing or no one else to be real. Yet, God is also the one who already knows who we really are, our True Self, our *haecceitas*. To love God as a sibling, spouse, or parent is, for St. Clare, the path to really knowing one's self and God.

The lesson St. Clare teaches us is to always return to the source of our real identity, not distracted as we so often are by the passing interests and things of everyday life but instead to contemplate who we are before God. In her third letter to Agnes of Prague, St. Clare offers this meditation that continues to speak to us today.

> Place your mind before the mirror of eternity!
> Place your soul *in the brilliance of glory!*
> Place your heart *in the figure of the* divine *substance*
> and, through contemplation,
> *transform* your entire being *into the image*

of the Godhead Itself,

so that you may feel what friends feel

in tasting *the hidden sweetness*

that, from the beginning,

God Himself has reserved for His lovers.

And, after all who ensnare their blind lovers

in a deceitful and turbulent world

Have been completely passed over,

May you totally love Him

Who gave Himself totally for your love,

At Whose beauty the sun and the moon marvel,

Whose rewards and their uniqueness and grandeur have no limits;

I am speaking of Him,

The Son of the Most High,

Whom the Virgin brought to birth

and remained a virgin after his birth.[5]

Like St. Clare, St. Francis, Thomas Merton, and John Duns Scotus, may
we strive ever more to become dunces in a world of False Selves. In
finding who it is we really are, uncovering our True Self, as it were, we
ultimately find God. For it is God who loved, created, and sustains us in
our very individuality and uniqueness.

Important Points to Remember

- All of creation is inherently contingent and beautiful, reflecting God's
  loving desire to create each and every aspect of the cosmos.
- God first loves you and me for who we are, as we are, before loving
  some generic idea of humanity or creation in general. God had always
  loved you and willed you into being.

- Every person has dignity and value regardless of who he or she is or what he or she has done.
- Before you can have a good relationship with someone else, you must first know yourself. We come to know our True Selves by coming to know God.
- One of the greatest challenges for this and future generations is to distinguish the True Self from the False Self or Digital Self.
- St. Clare of Assisi reminds us of how we must give up our False Selves and preoccupations with worldly things in order to find our True Selves in God.

Reflection Questions

1. What makes me unique among other human beings? What characteristics define who I am?

2. What do I bring to a relationship with another person? When I look inside myself, do I see my True Self? Do I look to find who I am in my relationship with God, or do I try to find or even *create* my identity on my own?

3. When have I not been true to my True Self? What motivated or prompted me to change? What pulls me back to my true identity?

4. Who is my Digital Self? How do my efforts to connect digitally with others affect my True Self, my False Self?

chapter three

✳

THE LONG-DISTANCE RELATIONSHIP
Loneliness

I call, I cling, I want—and there is no One to answer—no One on
Whom I can cling—no, No One.—Alone. The darkness is so dark—
and I am alone.—Unwanted, forsaken.—The loneliness of the heart
that wants love is unbearable....

In spite of it all—this darkness & emptiness is not as painful
as the longing for God.
—Mother Teresa of Calcutta[1]

Prayer and Loneliness

"My God, My God, why have you forsaken me?"

If Jesus Christ, whom we believe to be the Son of God, could express
abandonment, loneliness, and suffering, why wouldn't we? It's hard to
reconcile the experience and pain of loneliness in the spiritual life with
our understanding of a loving God. Some popular conceptions of the
spiritual life lead us to believe that if we are good and if we are open to
God then we will feel God's presence in our lives. Sometimes that's true.
Sometimes it's not. One thing that a closer look at the Christian tradition reveals to us is that even when we are good and are open to God,
we may very well still feel distant from God or lonely. What does our
prayer look like in those times?

If prayer is a way of living in the world, a position or stance that is ongoing communication with God in relationship, then what sort of experience is it when God seems distant? I would suggest that those periods in our lives when God feels distant and we feel alone are like a long-distance relationship. All long-distance relationships are difficult—sometimes very difficult. Even the mention of the term can really freak some people out. Such relationships can be scary and play into some of our worst insecurities. Long-distance relationships can seem to require a lot of effort, sometimes much more than if the other person was within arm's reach. Long-distance relationships (far too often) seem to make us do crazy or stupid things. And long-distance relationships test our emotions (and patience) in ways other experiences of dating simply do not.

Communication, which is at the heart of every type of relationship, takes on very different forms in a long-distance relationship. When you are dating someone from afar you have to rely on phone calls, e-mails, text messages, Skype chats, and maybe even those old-fashioned hand-written letters to express yourself and share your life with another. You have to be much more reliant on the spoken and written word to communicate, and it is only when you are limited to those modes of sharing that you come to realize how really important it is to be in the presence of the other.

This is one reason why we cannot say that prayer is just about "speaking" to God. At best, such a relationship amounts to what we might imagine is a good long-distance relationship. But as even those who, by choice or necessity, are in *good* long-distance relationships can attest, even good situations of the sort aren't that *great*. When we love another (a spouse, partner, friend, or sibling) we naturally desire to be with that person and to be close to him or her. But like all human relationships, our relationship with God is frequently less than perfect. And at times, by no intention of our own, we find that we are suddenly in a situation that seems a lot like a bad long-distance relationship with God. And it can be very lonely. What's worse is that God doesn't do e-mail, late-night phone calls, or video chats. On those occasions when we do send out those types of communication addressed to God, it can seem as though we get no response in return. And then what?

The Challenge of Loving from Afar

There are several ways that we can react in a situation that resembles a long-distance relationship with God. One way is to panic and walk away. When I was a senior in high school, I was dating a girl whom I liked very much. If I do say so, we were a cute couple and our classmates all seemed to think that we were perfect for each other (we were both voted "best personality" in the senior yearbook). As the year quickly came to a close and graduation was just a little more than a week away, I panicked. We were both going to different colleges that were more than four hours away from our hometown, in opposite directions. Knowing that such a relationship would be very hard and unsure of how to proceed, I broke up with her the week before graduation (not a very nice graduation gift to give to the valedictorian). I'm sure there were other emotional issues involved, but the overwhelming impulse was to bail in the face of a long-distance relationship. I just couldn't handle it.

It seems that this is a very common reaction for many people who feel loneliness or distance in their relationship with God. *"This is too hard, too confusing, too uncertain—I'm out of here!"* We all know people in this category. Maybe we are that person. Things become difficult in life and I no longer feel God's closeness as I once had. Perhaps I experience the loss of a loved one, a child, or a parent. Perhaps I lose my job or experience some sort of tragedy. I know that's when I bail and try to live as if God doesn't exist. It's when I say that the distance is just too much, too painful, and I will pretend this relationship never happened.

The same sort of situation is true with friends, but we usually don't cut ties so dramatically. How often do we come to realize (usually after the fact) that making a long-distance friendship work is a lot harder than we at first thought? Friends from high school, college, or work, even the closest of friends, have the tendency to drift away into the ocean of noncommunication. It happens for a number of reasons. Its cause can be blamed on both people, but the bottom line is that I—ultimately—decide that staying in touch, reaching out, picking up the phone is no longer worth it. It's a gradual loss, and we usually don't realize it until it's too late.

Like giving up on God, drifting away is not the best solution when we're faced with what feels like a long-distance relationship with God, and avoiding that takes effort (as any relationship does). It means being particularly attentive to the way God works in your life. It means being deliberate about what you choose to do with your time and energy. It means remaining open to the relationship itself and not succumbing to the temptation to take the easy way out, as we so often do with friends and family members who are difficult to stay in touch with. Drifting away is particularly common for those who stop going to church. I hate to sound like your grandmother, but going to church and celebrating the collective life of the community in giving glory to God is one way to be sure that God stays in your horizon and doesn't drift out to sea.

Another way to handle the long-distance relationship is to persevere like my brother and his girlfriend. They have been dating for several years. They met in college, and after graduation they both moved back to their respective hometowns to work, more than two hours away from each other. They don't see each other often, at least as often as a couple who might live in the same city, but they each try their hardest to stay in contact, to let the other know they are loved and thought of, even if they don't have the same instant gratification that in-person communication that comes from being in the same place at the same time provides. It's not easy, both of them can tell you that, but they are deliberate about how they share their lives with one another. There is a loneliness when they are physically apart, but the way they handle the distance is with trust and hope. They trust in each other's enduring commitment and hope that they will be able to experience each other in a more concrete way in the future.

This last way to approach long-distance relationships, with trust and hope, is particularly helpful for those of us who experience an absence of or distance from God. The psalms are filled with the laments of Israel, God's own chosen people, crying out to God, who appears to them to be absent. In fact, the words of Jesus on the cross—"My God, my God, why have You forsaken me?" come from Psalm 22. It's OK to be frustrated, saddened, or angry with God when God seems absent or far away. Just as it's OK to feel the same way about a loved one who is separated from you by a long distance. The first move, like so many other first steps, has to be one of coming to terms with the feelings and owning the experience. The psalms of lament show us one very integrated and honest way to express the suffering that feelings of abandonment and distance evoke. But like my younger brother and his girlfriend in their experience of their long-distance relationship, the Israelites learned to express their suffering in a spirit of trust and hope. Take Psalm 22, for example. It begins as a tortuous psalm of lament.

> My God, my God, why have you forsaken me?
> Why are you so far from helping me, from the words of my
> groaning?

O my God, I cry by day, but you do not answer;
and by night, but find no rest. (Psalm 22:1–2)

It's filled with illustration of suffering and misery, without much sign of relief. God is absent to the author of the psalm and there lies little consolation ahead; even when the narrator cries out to God, there is no answer. The self-worth of the author of the psalm seems to be dramatically affected by this loneliness, as when the author continues:

But I am a worm, and not human;
scorned by others, and despised by the people.
All who see me mock at me;
they make mouths at me, they shake their heads;
"Commit your cause to the LORD; let him deliver —
let him rescue the one in whom he delights!" (Psalm 22:6–8)

This feeling of the diminishing of self-worth is oftentimes what we feel when we are in a long-distance relationship and our loneliness gets the best of us. The way that relationship affects our self-perceptions bleeds over into the other relationships in our lives. We become overly sensitive to what we feel is scorn from others, or we might feel abandoned, despised, or ignored by others. Our whole world, like the author of this psalm, might feel empty and without hope.

Yet, the psalm continues, and after several verses that rehearse the intense and brutally honest ownership of the feelings of abandonment, there is a shift in tone. The psalm concludes with expressions of trust and hope. The author of the psalm begins to remember God's love and how in the past God delivered on the promise to always be there for Israel.

But you, O LORD, do not be far away!
O my help, come quickly to my aid!

Deliver my soul from the sword,
   my life from the power of the dog!
Save me from the mouth of the lion!

From the horns of the wild oxen you have rescued me.
I will tell of your name to my brothers and sisters;
   in the midst of the congregation I will praise you:
You who fear the LORD, praise him!
   All you offspring of Jacob, glorify him;
   stand in awe of him, all you offspring of Israel!
For he did not despise or abhor
   the affliction of the afflicted;
he did not hide his face from me,
   but heard when I cried to him. (Psalm 22:19–24)

The psalm reveals both a growing trust that God will do likewise in this difficult time and a hope that God will "return" soon. In anticipation of God's saving help, the author of the psalm promises to proclaim the wondrous power of God for generations to come, to be attentive to God's presence in the future, and to share with others the experience of suffering and relief.

Francis of Assisi, Mother Teresa, and Our Psalms

There are very few instances of St. Francis writing about his experience of God as distant or unresponsive. Then again, we have only about thirty small texts by the saint, most of which are less autobiographical and more intended for a particular audience with a particular theme. But we do have at least one insightful collection of writings by St. Francis that help us glimpse into this particular part of his spirituality. Like the people of Israel, St. Francis wrote his own psalms. He basically cut and pasted snippets from the Hebrew psalms but arranged them in a new collage of his own prayer. The collection of personal psalms has come to be called St. Francis's "Office of the Passion." Interested as he was about more and more faithfully entering into the mystery of Christ's passion, death, and resurrection, St. Francis composed a series of psalms that allowed him to express his spiritual experience after the model of Jesus Christ.

The first several psalms are very reminiscent of Psalm 22. In fact, St. Francis actually takes some selections from that particular psalm for use in constructing his own work. Take, for example, the beginning verses of his Psalm 6:

> O all you who pass along the way
> > look and see if there is any sorrow like my sorrow.
> For many dogs surrounded me
> > a pack of evildoers closed in on me.
> They looked and stared at me;
> > they divided my garments among them
> > and they cast lots for my tunic.
> They pierced my hands and my feet
> > they counted all my bones.
> They opened their mouth against me
> > like a raging and roaring lion.
> I have been poured out like water
> > and all my bones have been scattered.
> My heart has become like melting way
> > in the midst of my bosom.
> My strength has been dried up like baked clay
> > and my tongue clings to my jaws.[2]

What this seems to reveal is that, in his relationship with God, St. Francis, like all of us, struggled with periods of time that led him to feel overwhelmed by sorrow, abandoned by God, or distant from his

Creator. He certainly has the ability to articulate an experience like that viscerally. But the story doesn't end there. St. Francis, like the author of Psalm 22, always ends on a note of trust and hope. Sometimes it is as little as two lines, like the end of St. Francis's Psalm 6:

> *Blessed be the Lord, the God of Israel*
> *Who has redeemed the souls of His servant*
> with His very own most holy Blood
> *and Who will not abandon all who hope in Him.*
> And we know that *He is coming*
> *that He will come to judge justice.*[3]

Other times there is a significant or dramatic shift in the prayer, a shift reflected in the flow and movement of St. Francis's psalm.

The movement toward trust and hope can begin only with an honest engagement with our real feelings of loneliness, abandonment by, or distance from God. The Holy Spirit does work in and through us in ways that are at times hard to see. But the engagement with our feelings that come from a long-distance relationship with God can begin to free us to see signs of trust and hope. Like the author of Psalm 22, St. Francis models for us a way to respond to the dark periods of our spiritual lives.

One contemporary example of someone who experienced the pain of feeling distant from or abandoned by God is Mother Teresa of Calcutta. The Nobel Peace Prize laureate, holy woman on the path to official sainthood and all around symbol of selfless Christian service, suffered most of her life from what we might call a *very* long-distance relationship with God. When selections of her private writings were published in the 2007 book *Come Be My Light: The Private Writings of the "Saint of Calcutta,"* many people, including news reporters, were shocked by the discovery that this saintly woman who had so radically impacted our world for the better felt a lack of God's presence. "Surely," many of us thought, "Mother Teresa must have been living the radiant presence of God her whole life!" How else could such a person live the lifestyle she did, serving the poorest of the poor in the most inhumane conditions on earth?

The scandal of this revelation isn't so much that Mother Teresa felt as though she was removed from God's presence but that she continued to live a life of prayer and service on behalf of others *despite* that ongoing experience. If we are honest, we can identify periods in our lives when Mother Teresa's words of desire for God and feelings of abandonment ring true.

> Lord, my God, who am I that You should forsake me? The child of your love—and now become the most hated one—the one You have thrown away as unwanted—unloved.... My God—how painful is this unknown pain. It pains without ceasing. I have no faith. I dare not utter the words and thoughts that crowd in my heart—and make me suffer untold agony. So many unanswered questions live within me—I am afraid to uncover them.... If there be God, please forgive me. Trust that all will end in Heaven with Jesus. When I try to raise my thoughts to heaven—there is such convicting emptiness that those very thoughts return like sharp knives and hurt my very soul. Love—the word—it brings nothing. I am told God loves me—and yet the reality of darkness and coldness and emptiness is so great that nothing touches my soul.[4]

What makes her story and experience so important for us, however, is that, like the author of Psalm 22 and St. Francis, she didn't bail in her relationship with God and she didn't let God slip away like a friend out of touch but persevered in expressing her cries of suffering and loneliness, moving toward a spirit of trust and hope. Such is the case when she wrote, "Sometimes I find myself saying 'I can't bear it any longer' with the same breath I say 'I am sorry, do with me what you wish.'"[5] In the midst of the misery brought about by the feelings of loneliness and confusion, Mother Teresa still trusted and hoped that God was there, somewhere.

We too can write our own psalms of lament and express our prayers of suffering. In a journal or spoken aloud, our cries of abandonment and loneliness should come out. Like Jesus and St. Francis, we too might find in the ancient psalms of Israel the words we need to articulate our feelings, or we might find them in the contemporary writings of someone like Mother Teresa. Perhaps the words that reflect the sorrow of our heart can come only from our own depths, and maybe they can come out only in forms of music or art or dance. These small steps of prayerful beginning are a movement toward trusting and hoping that God has not abandoned us. Whatever the cause of that experience of long-distance relationship might be, and there are many reasons, most of which we might never understand, we can trust that the One we are in relationship with is still there loving us, and we can hope that we will feel that presence again.

Important Points to Remember

- Sometimes our relationship with God looks a lot like a long-distance relationship, when God's presence feels distant and our insecurities and fears take hold of our prayer.
- There are several ways to respond to the experience of feeling God's distance. We can choose to walk away and try to ignore God, or we can, with trust and hope, remain committed in our relationship, even during the difficult times.

- Francis of Assisi, Mother Teresa of Calcutta, and the author of Psalm 22 all show us ways to express the feelings of suffering and abandonment we might experience at some point in our relationship with God.
- Following the model of the psalms of lament, we can construct our own prayers that express our suffering.

Reflection Questions

1. When have I felt lonely? What were the circumstances and how did I get through this period of loneliness?

2. What are or have been the long-distance relationships in my life? How did I feel and act during these relationships?

3. Have I ever felt like I was in a long-distance relationship with God? How was that time similar to or different from my other experiences of long-distance relationship?

4. What are the challenges of being in a long-distance relationship? How have I met these challenges? What, if any, are the benefits of a long-distance relationship?

5. Besides those persons mentioned in this chapter, who are contemporary examples of people who feel abandoned by others and by God? What were their situations and any resolutions to their feelings of abandonment?

chapter four

Making a Date With God

Solitude

Now there was a great wind, so strong that it was splitting mountains and breaking rocks in pieces before the Lord, but the Lord was not in the wind; and after the wind an earthquake, but the Lord was not in the earthquake; and after the earthquake, a fire, but the Lord was not in the fire; and after the fire a sound of sheer silence. When Elijah heard it, he wrapped his face in his mantle and went out and stood at the entrance of the cave.

—1 Kings 19:11–13

Time to Be Alone

At first the difference can be hard to see. Being alone seems a lot like loneliness. And why wouldn't it? From an early age we've seen how being by one's self is often used as a form of punishment. "Go to your room!" our parents might have said when we did something wrong. It is no wonder that solitude is a scary experience when, from the earliest time of our youth, time alone—or "time out"—was perhaps one of the most common consequences of our frivolous childhood shenanigans. Though time out was nothing compared to the dreaded "grounding," which not only required solitude but also limited one's use of technology like the Internet, telephone, and television. And is it not curious that in our modern prison systems and educational programs the final recourse is forced solitude by means of ostracism under the forms of solitary confinement or the principal's office? Therefore it may not be surprising that the idea of spending time in solitude secluded from the modern world evokes mixed feelings.

It certainly did for me!

When I was a novice my classmates and I went to eastern Pennsylvania during the frigid cold of winter to spend ten days in solitude. I should explain that a novice is someone in religious life who spends an intense year learning about the tradition of the religious order, living in community, and praying and reading a lot but who has not yet professed religious vows. Some people like to say that the novitiate year is like "spiritual boot camp" for men and women in religious life. It's typically the beginning of one's path toward becoming a permanent member of a religious community.

My novice master announced to us that we would take part in a hermitage experience. We would spend our time alone, each in a small cabin, or hermitage, praying and reading. For someone like me, who loves being around people, having conversations, and interacting with others, the thought of several days with little or no contact with another human being was frightening. As it turned out, we would all gather together in the evening for about an hour to celebrate Mass and have dinner. The remaining twenty-three hours were for solitude. Before I left for the hermitage, my greatest fear was that I would be lonely. I didn't yet understand the difference between loneliness and being alone. Looking back at that time, I believe that a lot of that anxiety came from not understanding what prayer, contemplation, and solitude were all about.

In the last chapter we looked at what it means to experience loneliness in our spiritual life, something that can feel an awful lot like a long-distance relationship. While such periods in our life are painful, we know that there are ways to respond to those situations to keep the relationship alive even when we feel abandoned or lost. One thing that we come to realize in those moments of loneliness is how much we desire and need to be in the presence of those with whom we are in a relationship. In our relationships with other people, we know that we have to set aside time to be alone with another. Maybe we call it "date night" or just "our time." No matter how we describe it, we understand that it is a special time, a deliberate time, and a necessary time to keep the relationship healthy. What I came to realize while in the hermitage in the middle of the snowy Pennsylvania forest was that I was on a date with God.

Making a Date With God

It is fair to say that if you never spend time with another person you would be hard pressed to justify describing yourself as being in relationship with the other. In order to foster a healthy and meaningful relationship with someone, time must be set aside during which the other person is your focus and your presence to each other takes priority. Understandably, such an effort can be a challenge. With all of the distractions of life and the pressures of work and society, it seems nearly impossible and, more often than not, improbable that time can be made just to be and to be with another. It is particularly easy today to find distractions everywhere. Oftentimes we bring them with us, like the couple at the restaurant who spent an entire evening focused on their respective BlackBerry phones instead of the other person. It also seems that there are more demands placed on people today. I think of the myriad time commitments that even children and teenagers have these days: school, soccer practice, piano lessons, karate, classmate birthday parties, homework, play practice, and on and on. We simply *do* way too much.

This difficulty in finding time and space to really be present to another seems to occur much more frequently in a relationship that is taken for granted or in a complacent relationship that has been relegated to a lower status on one's priority list. As time goes on there are certain people, perhaps even people we love very much, who no longer receive the sort of attention from us that they once had. This experience is different from the time when we first begin to know a person. In romantic relationships we call this time dating. Dates are specific times reserved solely for experiencing the presence of another, to learn about him or her and to build a history of shared experiences. Transcending the stereotype of the romantic encounter, an experience like dating can be found in all types of relationships. When we first get to know our new friends, we want to spend time exclusively with them, we desire to be around them, and we wish to know all about them. We want to include these new and exciting people in all of our activities.

It's easy to make the effort to be alone with the other person. Dating can be like a superpower that provides us with energy, like the Energizer Bunny, to keep going and going. We have the strength and conviction to make all sorts of sacrifices for the other person, giving up our own time for another, thinking of somebody else before ourselves. This experience of relationship can make us feel like a sailboat out on a lake during a summer afternoon—we are gliding through life smoothly. But what happens when we've been sailing for a long time, let's say for months, and the lake begins to freeze? The smooth sailing begins to disappear. Our experience of the relationship is no longer quite as easy as it once was.

As time goes on and the friendship becomes more established, life more busy, and work more burdensome, what once was natural and easy requires planning and intention. Maintaining a relationship, romantic or otherwise, requires effort. It seems that many times, as a relationship matures, the effort it requires is mistaken for an absence of love. Love, it seems, is something that is associated with the effortless energy and attraction that comes with getting to know somebody new for the first time. Instead, what really happens is that the novelty of the person wears off and, in our culture, which emphasizes instant gratification, few people have the patience to work on a serious relationship.

The purpose of a hermitage experience is to set aside a time and create a space for solitude. One way to look at solitude is to consider it as you and another person spending time together alone, away from distractions, just the two of you. The only difference is that the other in this case is God. The hermitage helps provide the environment for such an encounter. By oneself in a small cabin, one finds no television to entertain, Internet to distract, or music to soothe. While out in the hermitages, my fellow novices and I followed the "Rule for Hermitages" that St. Francis wrote just for these occasions. Solitude was an important dimension of St. Francis's life. He knew that he had to balance his relationship with God with the demands of a life of work and ministry among those in society who were the most vulnerable and marginalized. He had to be deliberate in setting aside time and space, and he wanted those men and women who would follow his example of Christian life to do likewise. So St. Francis looked to the gospel to find a model for how to enter into solitude. He found his primary inspiration in the story of Jesus's visit to the house of his friends Martha and Mary.

> Now as they went on their way, he entered a certain village, where a woman named Martha welcomed him into her home. She had a sister named Mary, who sat at the Lord's feet and listened to what he was saying. But Martha was distracted by her many tasks; so she came to him and asked, "Lord, do you not

care that my sister has left me to do all the work by myself? Tell her then to help me." But the Lord answered her, "Martha, Martha, you are worried and distracted by many things; there is need of only one thing. Mary has chosen the better part, which will not be taken away from her." (Luke 10:38–42)

Adapting the Gospel passage of Jesus' encounter with Martha and Mary into a model for life at a hermitage, St. Francis designated half of the friars to take the role of Martha and the other half the role of Mary. Those Marthas look after the needs of the Marys by preparing the meals, planning the prayer and protecting the solitude of the Marys. Halfway through the experience the friars switch roles. St. Francis's instructions are very brief:

> Let those who wish to stay in hermitages in a religious way be three brothers or, at the most, four; let two of these be "the mother" and have two "sons" or at least one. Let the two who are "mothers" keep the life of Martha and the two "sons" the life of Mary and let one have one enclosure in which each one may have his cell in which he may pray and sleep.
>
> And let them always recite Compline [the last prayer] of the day immediately after sunset and strive to maintain silence, recite their Hours [of prayer], rise for Matins [Morning Prayer], and *seek first the kingdom of God and His justice.*[1]

This was the plan of action. Half of us would spend half the time serving as the Marthas, or "Mothers," and then we would switch roles. The idea being that one serves his brother so as to provide an environment without distractions for the one praying. It can be very easy for the Marys, when faced with the challenge of being alone with God, to say, "Oh, I better get dinner started," or, "Oh, I should really wash the dishes." St. Francis removed that distraction by having the Marthas take care of the everyday tasks. This way those in the hermitages are entirely free to be with God. After serving my brothers in the role of Martha, my time came to go off to the hermitage.

My Time in the Hermitage

The hermitage was not a bad place at all. Imagine one very large room with a tall ceiling, a space big enough for a bed, a little table, a reading chair, and a lamp. Picture then a small kitchenlike area for preparing meals and washing dishes, and a bathroom with a small shower stall. That's it. With no TV, no radio, no computer, no iPod, no cell phone, and no traffic (remember, we're in the middle of the woods), it was quiet. Very quiet. The thing about silence for those unfamiliar with it, especially for members of the Millennial generation or those who are extroverts or come from living in the city, is that it can be very scary. At first it feels isolating, like solitary confinement or time out. Then there are the problems associated with existence. That's right, I said existence. *If there is no one around to talk to or to speak to me, how do I confirm that I actually exist?* Sounds silly? The next time you change your Facebook status or Tweet and then wait around for people to "like" or comment, think again about these feelings of isolation. We're in an era when we crave and almost depend on external affirmation of our thoughts, feelings, and perspectives. *If a tree falls in the woods and no one is around to Tweet it, does it make a sound?*

The first day was really hard. I tried to occupy my mind with reading. In other words, I tried to distract myself from the reason I was really there. The reading kept me calm, for at least a while. But it didn't take all that long for me to acknowledge my feeling of isolation and, responding instinctively to the feeling of cabin fever, I bundled up to go outside for a walk in the snow-covered woods. Something happened out in those woods.

It was not long in the silence of the solitude that I understood I was not alone. Without even a book to distract me, I was out in creation surrounded by the stillness of a cold afternoon in the Pennsylvania forest. As I walked along a snowy trail I became aware that I was not *actually* by myself. Part of what jogged my attention was the beauty of creation and the rich feeling that I was not some spectator who had shown up like a patron at a zoo, peeking around at the surroundings like someone apart from and different from what was on display. Instead, I was sensitive to the reality of connectedness to all that was around me. The snow that lay on the ground provided insulation for the earth, the animals burrowed beneath the ground, and the plants that rested until spring. It would melt with the change of seasons and bring life-giving water that provided the very conditions for the plants to grow and rejuvenate the environment with life. Animals sought shelter in the forest and were nourished by the plant life of the woods. Even I became aware of the deeply intimate way in which I was dependent on the plants that inhaled my carbon dioxide and provided me with fresh oxygen in an exchange of breath and energy. And as if I were looking at a painting and had become suddenly aware of the artist who was responsible for its creation, I came to think about the source of this creation. Then, I came to sense the presence of that Divine Artist whose work was my very life and world. God didn't just create and hang the masterpiece in an art gallery but continued to always already be present to the very work lovingly designed for creation. God was with me in the forest, not like another human person could have been with me in the forest, but there with me all the same.

With all of the initial awkwardness of seeing a friend for the first time in a long time, I realized I was on a date with God.

How often have we found ourselves in that situation where, having lost touch with someone or having met someone for the first time, we are compelled to ease into conversation with small talk and innocuous chatting? The weirdness of the unknown, the embarrassment of having lost touch, and the uncertainty of how we are going to be received all contributes to this conversational tiptoeing. Being so accustomed to that sort of situation, I felt all the normal emotions and experienced all the normal thoughts that go along with that sort of reconnection, even though the one I was aware of wasn't like what I experienced with my other long-lost friends.

Soon I began to acknowledge that the awkwardness of this date was not mutual. God, like a patient and understanding friend, was simply present and comfortable with me. I was the only one who was uncomfortable. Burdened with self-consciousness and doubt, projecting my own insecurities and self-judgments on God, I found myself in a state of nervous confusion. It was not until I continued my walk in the woods that I realized, as if I were with a best friend or on a wonderful date, my presence was all God desired. In turn, God's presence was enough to calm my nerves, to assure me of my value and my ability to be loved. I experienced a form of transcendence while walking among and as part of creation with my Creator.

The Importance of Solitude

The concept of dating God is not new. Throughout history solitude has been sought to better hear the quiet, gentle voice of God. A close look at the narratives of God's ongoing relationship with humanity in both the Hebrew and the Christian Scriptures reveals solitude as the place of encounter with the God that is—as the history of God's chosen people, Israel, reveals—more and more a God for us. While in a cave awaiting the Lord, Elijah did not find God in the heavy wind, earthquake, or fire but in a tiny whisper (1 Kings 19:11–13). Today we do not find the Lord in the Internet, TV, or radio but in the quiet of time set aside for God.

This is not to suggest that solitude is the only way to experience God. Instead, it is a particular time, a dedicated time, a necessary time for a healthy relationship with God. Similarly, time alone with another is not the only form of dating. We find God in community with our sisters and brothers, in the activities of work or leisure and in art. While it is joyful and enriching to go on a date with someone to a movie, art gallery, or professional basketball game, it is difficult to enter into intimate conversation at that time. We might find that we are too distracted and our attention is divided by our surroundings. We might also indirectly take that opportunity to avoid facing the issues that we really need to address with God. Some dates with God will be experienced in liturgy, faith sharing, friendship, music, and other community events of our everyday life. However, there is a fundamental need to create a space and set aside a time that is just for God and where a deeper conversation can take root.

Jesus found close friendship with men and women of his day. He often chose to spend time with his friends, visiting with such folks while traveling around during his years of ministry. At other times he joined the larger community to teach, heal, or share a meal. We also know that Jesus frequently withdrew into solitude. After his baptism, and "filled with the holy spirit," Jesus returned from the Jordan and was led by the Spirit into the desert for forty days (see Matthew 4:1; Mark 1:12; Luke 4:1). We read that it was the custom of Jesus to go and pray on the Mount of Olives (Luke 22:39). When we answer the call to "follow me" (see Luke 5:27; John 1:43), we follow Jesus to the Father in solitude. Jesus shows us that in solitude we are never alone but that solitude is the privileged location of our encounter with God. We are with our Creator to Whom we are the beloved children created in God's image.

Dating God does not require a hermitage any more than taking a spouse on a date requires a special destination. Solitude comes when we create the space and set aside the time to enter more deeply into the mystery that is the very Love that gives us life and meaning. It can be found in the quiet of the morning before the busy day, in the ten-minute walk at lunch, or in the restful moments before bed. Just as with creating time and space to be alone with another person, creating time and space for solitude is more about intentionality and the desire to be fully present in the moment than it is about being in this or that location.

While solitude may appear scary at first, confronting that fear is perhaps the first step to deepening one's relationship with God. Just as the prospect of learning more about another person or ourselves can be daunting, the reward comes in the connection that is formed when two know each other in the openness of an intimate friendship. Going into the created space and time set aside for solitude is going on a date with God.

Important Points to Remember

- While difficult to see at first, there is a difference between loneliness and being alone. Healthy relationships with others and with God require times of being alone with the other.
- The earliest stages of all relationships can seem effortless, but as time goes on healthy relationships, including those with God, require effort and patience that is more deliberate.
- A hermitage experience is simply one way to set aside time to be alone with God. One can create a hermitage experience in a variety of ways. Solitude comes when we create the space and set aside the time to

enter more deeply into the mystery that is the very Love that gives us life and meaning.

Reflection Questions

1. What is the difference between being lonely and being alone? When in my life have I been lonely? When have I been alone for a significant amount of time? Have I ever been alone but not lonely?

2. When I look at my daily and weekly routines, where in them do I find that I have time alone? Times of solitude and quiet? Do I want or crave more silence and solitude? How will I satisfy this desire or need?

3. When I am alone, do I speak to God? What do I say?

4. When I am alone, do I listen to God? What do I hear?

5. How can I create a hermitage experience? Do I need to make a date with God?

chapter five

Becoming an Everyday Mystic
Contemplation

We can contemplate God
not only outside us and within us
but also above us:
outside through his vestiges, within through his image
and above through the light
which shines upon our minds,
which is the light of Eternal Truth,
since "our mind itself is formed immediately by Truth itself."
—St. Bonaventure, *The Soul's Journey Into God*[1]

Being and Doing

I used to think that contemplation was something that we do, some*thing* like brushing your teeth or making coffee. I used to fear contemplation because, it seemed to me, at least, I wasn't very good at it. That is, I wasn't very good at doing what I thought contemplation was. I remember being in high school and going on a weekend retreat sponsored by my home diocese for young men who were thinking about a vocation to ordained ministry as priests. At the time I felt rather strongly that God wanted me to be a priest. During this retreat I remember being very frustrated that I couldn't pray as I thought I should be praying; that I wasn't contemplating the way I should be contemplating; that I wasn't *doing* what I thought I should be doing.

I had convinced myself that what it meant to pray on retreat was to engage in something like intense, private, meditative prayer that I envisioned being contemplation. I suppose that I imagined it to be a lot like what we might call centering prayer made popular in recent years by Trappist monk Fr. Thomas Keating, o.c.s.o. Contemplation was something you did in solitude, when on retreat, for example, and it looked and felt a certain way. This feeling of frustration about not being able to *do* contemplation correctly stayed with me for years. It wasn't until after I became a Franciscan postulant (someone in his first year of training to be a Franciscan friar) that my spiritual director at the time explained something to me that changed my life. He said, "Dan, centering prayer doesn't do it for everybody." He explained that there is no "one way" to pray and that to think I have to *do* something simply because I thought it is the way I was supposed to be doing it was misguided.

On one hand, I felt freedom from the burden of trying to conform to my own image of what prayer should look like. On the other hand, I felt ever more confused about how I should pray. The problem was I still had this static notion of what prayer was, and it took St. Bonaventure and Bl. Angela of Foligno to clue me in to what I should really be focused on. At the heart of my frustration and confusion was this preconceived idea I had about what someone "does" in contemplation. Although there are helpful guides and tools to assist people of faith to tune in to the presence of God, contemplation in the Franciscan tradition had little to do with a pattern or product and more to do with a way of being. *Who* you are and *how* you live, rather than *what* you do, is the real foundation for a life of prayer and contemplation. St. Francis even talks about this in several of his writings. When his brother friars ask him about what someone should do in life, Francis always responded with the idea that it doesn't matter *what* someone does as long as it doesn't extinguish the *spirit* of prayer and devotion to God. One way to look at this perspective is to say that we need to be less concerned with the things we do, or with the compartmentalization of our lives into this thing at this time and that thing at that time, and instead to work on becoming increasingly aware of God's presence in our lives at all times.

Earlier we looked at how prayer in the Franciscan tradition is about relationship. Like dating, the way we relate to God bears remarkable similarities to the ups and downs, joys and sorrows, the effortless and the more laborious expression of being close to another. In light of that view, contemplation cannot be awareness of God at this or that time but instead a movement toward an awareness of God at all times. I don't think that I'm alone in my previous frustration and confusion about the meaning of contemplation. It seems that lots of people have similar frustrating experiences with this conception of contemplation. Ilia Delio in her book *Franciscan Prayer* tells a story about a student who wrote in a paper that he never though he could strive for contemplation because "contemplation is for special people, not for the ordinary person like me."[2] Her response is that everyone is called to contemplation. If contemplation, then, is neither a particular way of praying, as I thought, nor, as Delio's student thought, reserved only for extraordinary people and saints, then what is it?

Seeing the World Anew

St. Francis of Assisi did not find God just in the extraordinary moments of life. Nor did he understand his experiences of God to be limited by select moments of intense prayer, although he certainly had those. What makes Francis so unique, so attractive to those who would follow his way of Christian living, is that he could see God in all things. The word *contemplation*, from the Latin *contemplatio*, means "to see, to gaze, to focus." Whereas I was once limited (and subsequently frustrated) by an understanding that contemplation, this seeing or focusing on God, had to take place in at a particular way and at a particular time, Francis shows us that the whole world and our whole life offer us this opportunity for contemplation.

If we think back to our relationships with others, we can talk a lot about what each person does, listing chores, jobs, and responsibilities and try to construct an understanding of who a person is, based on those data. Or, we can define a person by their relationships. What makes a husband a husband isn't a list of things a husband *does* but a relationship to his spouse. What makes a daughter a daughter is her relationship to her parents. What makes us who we are comes from our relationship with God, and that should shape the way we live in this world. I recently read a short article in the the *New Yorker* magazine about professional tennis players who are also parents of young children. One player had said that before becoming a father he was much more worked up about tournament losses. Now that he has a young child, he feels more calm and less shaken about winning or losing because, he said, he realizes there are more important things in this life and that winning or losing a tennis match is just not one of them. His whole outlook on life, about what he *does*, changed because of his relationship. No longer did he define himself by doing things—even great things—but instead he sees himself and his world in a new light because he is changed by his relationship as a father.

Contemplation in the Franciscan tradition can be a lot like the experience of conversion that this tennis player encountered when he entered into a new type of relationship. We saw in the last chapter that all relationships require time to be set aside, devoted to the other. Deliberately and consciously spending time alone with God is absolutely necessary, but we can't do that forever (even Franciscans have to leave the chapel every now and then!). What about those in-between times? Is contemplation, the seeing and focusing on God, limited to those datelike experiences of solitude? No, I don't think so.

When St. Bonaventure wrote about contemplation in his famous book *The Soul's Journey Into God*, he was deliberate in using the Latin word *speculatio* instead of *contemplatio*, the term so many other writers had used over the centuries. It may not seem like such a big deal, especially for English speakers because, in some cases, we have many words to describe similar things (take the many meanings of *love*, yet we have only one word), so nuances like this get lost. The root word for *speculatio* is *speculum*, which is a noun meaning "a mirror." Bonaventure, inspired by the life and example of St. Francis, understood contemplation to be about reflection. On one level it could mean reflection on God, like *contemplation*, the seeing or focusing on God. Yet, on a deeper level, St. Bonaventure is talking about the reflection of God in our world. He uses another Latin word to talk about how God is reflected in creation. He describes these instances as vestiges (*vestigia*), which literally means "footprints." (I bet you weren't expecting to learn so much about Latin in this book!)

St. Bonaventure says that God is reflected in every part of creation as if it were a footprint of God, as if God had left a personal mark on everything. This shouldn't be too surprising for us. Remember in chapter 2 when we talked about John Duns Scotus's view of everything being uniquely and individually loved into existence by God? The world reflects God, like a mirror, because God is in relationship with creation. What is significant for us is that Franciscan contemplation, then, is not about us searching high and low for God, concerned about seeing and focusing in just the right way and at the right time. No, Franciscan contemplation is about learning to see how God is always already right before us, reflected in all aspects of creation. We need to see the world anew, not because God is hidden and waiting for us to take our turn in spiritual hide-and-seek, but because God is always "it" and at play around us. God is not doing the hiding, God's footprints are everywhere. We are usually the ones hiding, not seeing or focusing, as it were, on what is right before us, but instead we are usually preoccupied with the unimportant things in life, like winning tennis matches or getting a promotion at work. We can't let contemplation, the gazing at God, become just another thing we have to do. We need to let our relationship with God transform us as a child transforms a tennis star into a father, who then sees the whole world in new and life-giving ways.

Early on in his *Soul's Journey Into God*, St. Bonaventure describes this problem of our tendency not to see God around us in our daily, ordinary lives. He believed that this is a common phenomenon and that all humans suffer from the same problem. He writes:

> In the initial state of creation, man was made fit for the quiet of contemplation, and therefore *God placed him in a paradise of delights* (Gen 2:15). But turning from the true light to changeable good, man was bent over by his own fault, and the entire human race by original sin, which infected human nature in two ways: the mind with ignorance and the flesh with concupiscence. As a result, man, blinded and bent over, sits in darkness and does not see the light of heaven unless grace with justice come to his aid against concupiscence and unless knowledge with wisdom come to his aid against ignorance.[3]

When bent over all we can see is ourselves. Original sin is another way of talking about our selfish tendency not to be concerned with others. Being bent over is also another way of talking about a distorted view of the world. Not only do we see ourselves in a distorted way, we certainly cannot see God and the rest of creation with a distorted worldview, let alone God *in* the rest of creation. When we are bent over and in darkness we are preoccupied with what we do and not who we are in relationship with others.

St. Bonaventure's solution is to allow Christ to raise us up. We need to cooperate with God's grace to lift our heads up and open our eyes to see the world around us. Then we can begin to examine creation and the everyday experiences of others as reflecting God. Then we might be reminded of who we are in relationship with God, and that will transform our worldview to what is important. Therefore we might follow Francis's example, not limited to seeing God in the occasional events of the extraordinary but seeing God in the ordinary.

Franciscan Contemplation, Franciscan Mysticism

Like St. Bonaventure, Bl. Angela of Foligno, a Third Order, or "secular," Franciscan, believed that all of creation reflected God. Instead of describing creation as a mirror or footprint of God, Angela saw the world as "pregnant with God." In her famous book *The Memorial*, Angela recounts to a friar scribe the events of her spiritual journey. At one point, Angela recalls attending Mass in Assisi during which she had a particularly powerful experience of God's presence. She heard God say to her, "My sweet daughter, no creature can give you this consolation, only I alone." Angela shares that this experience was one of great endearment and intimacy, it was a recognition of God's closeness to and care for her. She continued:

> Afterward [God] added: "I want to show you something of my power." And immediately the eyes of my soul were opened, and in a vision I beheld the fullness of God in which I beheld and comprehended the whole of creation, that is, what is on this side and what is beyond the sea, the abyss, the sea itself, and everything

else. And in everything that I saw, I could perceive nothing except the presence of the power of God, and in a manner totally indescribable. And my soul in an excess of wonder cried out: "This world is pregnant with God!" Wherefore I understood how small is the whole of creation—that is, what is on this side and what is beyond the sea, the abyss, the sea itself, and everything else—but the power of God fills it all to overflowing.[4]

For Angela, God's love and care for her were directly related to all of creation. Her ability to see God in all of creation—she explicitly attributes that to God's opening of her eyes to see the world as it *really* is: a sign of God's generous love. Angela provides us with another model of Franciscan contemplation, one that is also described as "mysticism." Theologian Richard McBrien explains that mysticism is that graced transformation of our awareness or consciousness that "follows upon a direct or immediate experience of the presence of God leading to a deeper union with God." He goes on to explain "that union, however, does not isolate the individual from others or from the world. The deep union achieved by Bernard of Clairvaux, Francis of Assisi, and Catherine of Siena, for example, led them into greater apostolic activity and into service of others."[5] Such was the case with Angela.

In many ways, Angela of Foligno was a woman of her age. Born around 1248, she came from a rather wealthy family and followed the pattern of life typical for a medieval woman: She married in 1270 and had several children. However, around 1288 her life took an unexpected and dramatic turn. Her entire family died—her children, husband, and mother. In the years prior to the deaths of her loved ones, Angela had become increasingly aware that the way she was living her life was not sufficient. She felt the burden of her own sinfulness and felt a strong desire to live a more prayerful, reflective life. After the deaths of her family members, Angela was drawn to follow the example of St. Francis of Assisi and live the rest of her life as a penitent—that is, someone who makes a public commitment to live in evangelical poverty, prayer, and service. Selling her property and using the money to help the poor in her town, Angela felt freed from the trappings of wealthy medieval life. Dedicated as she was now to follow St. Francis's way of life, her mode of prayer was that of Franciscan contemplation.

As we read in the passage above, Angela's personal outlook and worldview were dramatically impacted by her decision to live a life of prayer and poverty after the example of St. Francis. She began to see the world as it *really* was. She increasingly came to view creation and others as God views them. Her life of contemplation led to a deeper experience of God, and that, in turn, shaped her relationship with others. Angela's experience of God, in creation, in the world around her, is not something that is of her *doing* but instead something about her *being*. Mysticism understood as that close union with God is about being in relationship with God and creation in a new way that affects one's everyday life. Sure, there are times when we feel God's presence in our lives and world around us to greater or lesser degrees, but the possibility of experiencing that presence is not limited to a time or place at which we do this or that thing. Instead, as Franciscan friar Dennis Tamburello, O.F.M., reflecting on the place of contemplation and mysticism in the Christian life, said so well, "Mysticism—as intimacy with God—is ultimately something to be lived, not just studied. Our goal—which each of us will approach in a different way —is to respond to the gift of divine grace and so to become one spirit with God."[6]

The renowned Franciscan author and poet Murray Bodo, O.F.M., has reflected on the way in which this experience of mysticism, this intimacy with God, should be carried with us in a way that touches all of our lives.

The moment of ecstasy for all mystics is the moment of God's entrance into their lives, an experience so intense that they are aware of nothing except the infinity of God's love, and they want nothing but to submit themselves to the will of that love—the source of all bliss, of all fulfillment and enlightenment and peace. In order to keep attuned to that will, mystics are much concerned not to let preoccupation with self or with the material blind them. They are perpetually aware that their experience of God was completely gratuitous, that it was not merited but was pure grace. Though some are graced to have this experience more than once, it is not something that can be repeated at will; it must be lovingly recalled at all times, like a cherished and life-changing memory.[7]

In a sense, this experience of the divine in a deeply intimate way should help reshape our outlook on life, renewing in us a desire to live as Franciscan contemplatives, seeing the world anew.

The purpose of contemplation is to change who we are by allowing God to shape and influence the way we see reality. This is something that Christians need to embrace and live out every day, not just on this or that occasion or in this or that way. The more we become contemplatives in the Franciscan tradition, the more we can recognize those special moments of mystical encounter with our Creator. The result of living this way is, to quote the prayer that is so often associated with St. Francis, although he did not write it himself, that we are able to become ambassadors of God's peace. Where there is hatred, we can show love. Where there is injury, pardon; where there is despair, hope; where there is darkness, light; and where there is sadness, joy.

Important Points to Remember

- Contemplation in the Franciscan tradition is more than *something* we do, it is how we live with an awareness of God in the world. Contemplation has to do with relationship.
- St. Bonaventure teaches us that contemplation is recognizing the mirrors of God's love in all of creation and that true contemplation lifts us up from being bent down and focused on ourselves.
- Bl. Angela of Foligno viewed the world as "pregnant with God," full of possibility, and reminders of the Creator who loves everything into existence.
- The purpose of contemplation is to change who we are by allowing God to shape and influence the way we see reality.

Reflection Questions

1. What has been my experience with praying—as a child, as an adult? Has my way of praying changed as I have aged?
2. When in my life have I found it difficult to pray? What made praying difficult?
3. In what ways do I see God's love mirrored in my life, in the lives of others?
4. In what ways do I see the world differently because of my relationship with God?

chapter six

❋

LOVE LETTERS FROM GOD: THE WORD

The Sacred Scriptures, on the other hand, are most fittingly likened to a
honeycomb, for while in the simplicity of their language they seem dry,
within they are filled with sweetness.
—Hugh of St. Victor, *Didascalicon*[1]

The Story of God for Us

Everybody enjoys a good love story, particularly if it is romantic and
has a happy ending. This fact helps explain why, month after month,
Hollywood and television networks produce more and more romantic
and situation comedies. It might also explain the popularity of the cable
network TLC's programs *A Wedding Story* and *A Baby Story*. This truth
also sheds some light on why couples are asked by every new person
they encounter to "tell their story" (*How did you two meet?*).

We simply take great joy in the personal narrative of others and the
stories of their relationships. Perhaps this is why reading the love letters of others is so fascinating. In the introduction to his book *The 50
Greatest Love Letters of All Time*, a collection of romantic and touching
correspondence between some of the greatest historical figures of the
last several centuries, David Lowenhertz writes, "Sometimes nothing
speaks louder than a silent word written on a piece of paper."[2] He goes
on to explain that the act of writing, unlike some of our more speedy
forms of communication today, offers those communicating the chance

to reflect on the ways in which they wish to express the secrets of their hearts. To receive a love letter, a deeply touching and reflective expression of someone's true feelings for you and the description of your relationship that is contained in that letter, speaks to our hearts in indescribable ways. I don't believe that there is a more revealing way to understand one's story than through love letters.

A large part of this book has been dedicated to inviting you to imagine your relationship with God anew, to consider your prayer as a way of being-in-the-world, to set aside time for God by making a space for solitude and for committing yourself to a more contemplative life that challenges you to see the world in a new way. This, it has been suggested, comes with a renewed approach to Franciscan spirituality, an approach that models our conceptualization of our relationships with God as being like dating. To achieve this aim, it has been necessary to reconsider terms and images we've often associated with other definitions or meanings. Such is the case with Scripture.

Whatever your previous conception of Scripture may have been, I invite you to temporarily suspend that outlook. In light of the image of dating God, I suggest that we begin to consider Scripture as a story. What sort of story? The story of God's love for all of creation!

This notion of Scripture as the story of God's love for all of creation is not new, nor is it my invention. Instead it comes to us from the Bible itself. The way that Scripture came to be written down, shared, collected, and eventually organized into a canon originates with the telling of stories. Oral tradition is the source of Scripture's content, rooted of course in the Spirit's divine inspiration. Long before there was the written book of Genesis, the people of Israel spoke the truth of God's creative action and embrace of the world in language now recognizable as the beginning of the Hebrew Scriptures. One might imagine children and parents gathered around a small community's wisdom figure to hear about how the world came to be, to hear why human beings at times make bad choices and fall short of their potential, or to hear about God's personal covenant with humanity.

Those gathered together to share the collective story of God's love for creation might hear how God revealed to Moses God's very name, a name so holy it should not be said. A name signified by four letters, YHWH, which will come to be translated centuries later as "I am." But the hearers of this story would understand the complexities and richness of God's name, which is eventually lost in translation. It is a name that *describes* God, not limiting God as the more philosophical reading of "I am" so often does. A more accurate rendering of God's name in translation reads: "I am the one who will be there for you." It bespeaks relationship and future. It tells in miniature the whole story of God's relationship with humanity and all creation. When Moses goes to the pharaoh on behalf of God's people, he is to say that he is sent by the One who journeys with the chosen people. We see this in the often overlooked next verse in the book of Exodus, where, in another, more relational way, God explains to Moses who God is.

> God also said to Moses, 'Thus you shall say to the Israelites, "The Lord, the God of your ancestors, the God of Abraham, the God of Isaac, and the God of Jacob, has sent me to you":
> This is my name for ever,
> and this my title for all generations. (Exodus 3:15)

The name of God is precisely who God is, a God who is with us, who loves us and who will be there for us. This is made even clearer in the next line as God continues to speak to Moses.

> Go and assemble the elders of Israel, and say to them, "The Lord, the God of your ancestors, the God of Abraham, of Isaac, and of

Jacob, has appeared to me, saying: I have given heed to you and to what has been done to you in Egypt. I declare that I will bring you up out of the misery of Egypt, to the land of the Canaanites, the Hittites, the Amorites, the Perizzites, the Hivites, and the Jebusites, a land flowing with milk and honey." (Exodus 3:16–17)

When we don't just stop with "I am" but read on to hear God explain who God is to Moses, we come to see that God is concerned about us and the way we are treated. God is not some abstract deity but a creator who is head-over-heels in love with humanity and seeks what is best for creation out of that love and concern.

This is not the case in these three verses in Exodus but throughout all of Scripture. In both powerful and at times more subtle ways, God reveals who God is through Scripture, which is why we call it revelation. Revelation, at the most fundamental level, means relationship. When we talk about revelation we are always already talking about a speaker and a hearer. Someone must do the "revealing" or self-disclose, and another must be the "receiver" or hearer of that word. To talk about Scripture as divine revelation is to talk about a historical and religious text that mediates that ongoing relationship between the revealer (God) and the receiver (all of humanity). In other words, Scripture isn't just a book full of information one can consult, like a dictionary or an encyclopedia (or Wikipedia, for that matter), nor is it a history book or some work of fiction. It is the medium by which God's revelation or self-disclosure is passed down from one generation to the next.

If prayer is relationship, the dynamic communication of one's self to God, then Scripture might be something like love letters from God. Just as one person passes on, in an historical, tangible way, his or her feelings for the person he or she is dating so too the Christian community passes on the stories of the community's experience of God in an historical and tangible way. Just as you can come to know much about the relationship between two people by reading their love letters, so too we can learn a lot about our relationship with God and the history of that experience through Scripture. Just as there are a variety of forms such communication can take between those dating (poetry, art, prose, laundry lists of information, journals, and so on), so, too, Scripture conveys the experience of relationship with God in manifold ways.

Although the metaphor is less than perfect—as all metaphors for describing and relating to God are—viewing Scripture as "love letters from God" causes us to pause and reconsider the significance of the Bible in our personal and communal lives of faith. Have you ever thought of Scripture as a way to get to know God better? Or, has Scripture largely been a combination history/rule book? Thinking about the Word of God in terms of "love letters" personalizes Scripture in a way that draws us closer to what those earliest storytellers of the faith sought to express: God is the One who will be there for us, is concerned about us, and loves us. That's God's name, after all!

The Importance of Scripture for Francis

Although he never referred to Scripture as love letters from God, Francis certainly looked after Scripture with the care and devotion that we might show our most prized possessions. It can be difficult for modern people who are used to mass-produced paper (and digital text), living centuries after the invention of the printing press, to appreciate how important the written word was in Francis's time. Oftentimes the material needed to write a copy of a biblical book or the prayers for the Mass were difficult to acquire and expensive. Unlike our liturgical books and Bibles today, Scripture was often copied out on a variety of pages. These pages, usually unbound, had the tendency (as most loose papers do) to become scattered and lost. This happened even in churches.

Francis was concerned about the way these particles of Scripture were cared for (or, more accurately, not cared for). He was almost obsessed with making sure that all pieces of Scripture were well taken care of and treated with respect and dignity. In a letter addressed to the entire Order of Franciscans, Francis shares his vision of the importance of caring for Scripture in a command that all friars should go out of their way to gather, protect, and venerate even the most seemingly insignificant scriptural texts. He writes:

> Because *whoever belongs to God hears the words of God,* we who are more especially charged with divine responsibilities must not only listen to and do what the Lord says but also care for the vessels and other liturgical objects that contain His holy words in order to impress on ourselves the sublimity of our Creator and our subjection to Him. I, therefore, admonish all my brothers and encourage them in Christ to venerate, as best as they can, the divine written words wherever they find them. If they are not well kept or are carelessly thrown around in some place, let them gather them up and preserve them, inasmuch as it concerns them, honoring the words of the Lord *Who spoke them.* For many things are made holy by the words of God and the sacrament of the altar is celebrated in the power of the words of Christ.[3]

Francis did not see in the Word of God some removed and abstract sense of God's presence but recognized the truly intimate and life-giving quality of Scripture. We see this most strongly in the assertion that Francis makes before instructing his brothers to collect these pieces of Scripture, when he explains that it is Scripture that allows us to "impress on ourselves the sublimity of our Creator."

The God who is so oftentimes viewed as removed or absent or so totally other-than-us that we cannot possibly relate becomes accessible to us and close through Scripture. This is what Francis means when he says that God's sublimity becomes impressed on us through Scripture. Like a loved one's correspondence that we keep in a special place and treasure because it reveals some dimension of a person's heart and soul, these fragments of Scripture are seen by Francis as invaluable and demanding our care and attention.

Francis's whole way of life began with Scripture. When the time came to more formally organize what it means to live as a friar minor (a "lesser brother") in the world, Francis explained that "the Rule and Life of the Lesser Brothers is this: to observe the Holy Gospel of Our Lord Jesus Christ by living in obedience, without anything of one's own, and in chastity."[4] The saint's first biographer explains that even before Francis lived a more formal religious life, in the time commonly remembered as the period of Francis's "conversion," the young man became enthralled with a particular selection of passages from the Gospel as they were read in church.

> One day the gospel was being read in that church about how the Lord sent out his disciples to preach. The holy man of God, who was attending there, in order to understand better the words of the gospel, humbly begged the priest after celebrating the solemnities of the Mass to explain the gospel to him. The priest explained it all to him thoroughly line by line. When he heard that Christ's disciples should not *possess gold* or *silver* or *money,* or *carry on their journey a wallet or a sack, nor bread nor a staff,* nor *to have shoes* nor *two tunics,* but that they should preach *the kingdom of God* and *penance,* the holy man, Francis, immediately *exulted* in the *spirit of God.* "This is what I want," he said, "this is what I seek, this is what I desire with all my heart."

The holy father, *overflowing with joy*, hastened to implement the words of salvation and did not delay before he devoutly began to put into effect what he heard.[5]

Francis's desire was to follow in the footprints of Christ, to be open to the will of God as Christ was open to the will of God, and the way he was able to discern that path was in and through Scripture.

What we most want, what we most desire in our relationships with others is often conveyed in the romantic or poetic expressions of our heart to another. Thomas of Celano, in attempting to capture precisely this romantic quality in the desire of Francis to follow the Word of God, to live the gospel of Jesus Christ, puts it this way:

> People thought [Francis] wanted to get married, and they would ask him: "Do you want to get married, Francis?" He replied: "I will take a bride more noble and more beautiful than you have ever seen, and she will surpass the rest in beauty and excel all others in wisdom."
>
>
>
> Indeed
> the *unstained bride* of God is
> the true *religion* that he embraced,
> and the hidden treasure *the kingdom of heaven,*
> that he sought with great longing.
> For it had to be that the gospel call be fulfilled
> in the one who was to be
> *in faith and truth*
> *a minister of the Gospel.*[6]
>
>

To be a minister of the gospel means to be the servant of God's word. In practical ways, such as the gathering and protecting of scattered pieces of Scripture, Francis was indeed a servant of God's word. Yet, it was also in less explicit ways that Francis's way of life exhibited an openness to and an awareness of God's invitation to be in relationship. In his book *Hope Against Darkness: The Transforming Vision of Saint Francis in an Age of Anxiety,* Richard Rohr, a popular Franciscan writer, describes this aspect of Francis's life: "Francis's living of the gospel was just that: It was lifestyle pure and simple. It was the Incarnation continuing in space and time. It was the presence of the Spirit taken absolutely seriously. It was *being* Jesus more than simply worshiping him."[7]

How Francis allowed the Word of God to speak to his heart, much as we might allow the words of a loved one to touch ours, led him into a new way of living. No longer was it sufficient to go about being in the world as he once had, but instead he was changed by the relationship God had invited him to enter. What began as God's embrace of Francis in Creation became a life lived in response to the call of God to be in an increasingly intimate relationship. Therefore, it was no longer just OK to be a "hearer" of the Word. We must be "doers" of the Word. We must live a life of relationship in an active way, not just in a passive way, as the following in the letter of James instructs us:

> Be doers of the word and not merely hearers who deceive them-
> selves. For if any are hearers of the word and not doers, they
> are like those who look at themselves in a mirror and, on going
> away, immediately forget what they were like. But those who
> look into the perfect law, the law of liberty, and persevere, being
> not hearers who forget but doers who act—they will be blessed
> in their doing. (James 1:22–25)

Prior to living a life modeled after the gospel in spirit and action, Francis could reasonably consider himself in the camp of those of us who look into the mirror of life and promptly forget who we are and what we're about. But Scripture is the mirror of God's word, and to look into it is to look into the life and love of God. We don't look into Scripture and forget but instead recall the experience that is shared in the history of God becoming close to us, drawing near to us, and inviting us to be in relationship. While information, facts, and figures can be forgotten over time, experience stays with us and calls us out of the everyday to make the ordinary extraordinary and ultimately change our lives.

Love letters addressed to us have the capacity to convey more than mere facts and figures. Love letters evoke experience in the recipient, an experience of love that goes beyond simple words in ink on paper. Reading love letters can draw us out of ourselves to remember that we are in relationship with another, and the experience of reading those letters is more significant for the addressee than it could be for some other observer. That we are the addressees of God's love letters, which are the Word, makes us intimately connected to this experience and not just some passive observer of the correspondence. This experience, then, calls us to be doers and not just stay in the realm of readers removed from the content. As the letter of James says so well, the reader must become a doer of the word. The response to love letters is to return that love, live in a new way, and see the world through the eyes of love.

Like those letters we cherish from our loved ones, letters that call us to return to the experience of relationship with another and see the world differently, Scripture can change our lives. Approaching the Word of God as Francis did, as if they were love letters from God and so worthy of our most precious care, cannot end with our reading or hearing. No, we must become doers of the word, which is exactly what Francis did.

Living the "Love Letters from God"

The relationship that Francis had with Scripture was something special. It was, as we've already seen, the pattern and program for his way of life. It was also the concrete expression of who God was for Francis, and it was something so important that he took extra care to always protect it from harm or neglect. Yet, Francis was not simply one, like the "hearers" whom the letter of James talks about, to passively approach Scripture, but instead he was a fervent doer of the word. The way in which Francis was a doer gives us a model of what it means to live the love letters from God in our own day.

St. Bonaventure, the Franciscan friar who become the minister general of the Franciscan Order a few decades after the death of Francis, set out to write what was supposed to be "the definitive biography" of Francis. Taking the previous efforts to capture the life and story of the Saint from Assisi, Bonaventure wrote a richly illustrative and deeply spiritual depiction known today as *The Major Life of St. Francis*. (It's called "major" because Bonaventure also composed a "minor," or short, version of the saint's biography.)

At one point in his *Life of St. Francis*, Bonaventure describes the unique way in which the poor man from Assisi was able to understand the meaning of Scripture such that he astounded even the most learned and wise scholars of the day.

Unflagging zeal for prayer
with a continual exercise of virtue
had led the man of God to such serenity of mind that,
although he had no expertise in Sacred Scripture through learning,
his intellect, nevertheless
enlightened by the splendor of eternal light,
probed the depths of Scripture
with remarkable incisiveness.
For his genius, pure and unstained,
penetrated *hidden mysteries*,
and where the knowledge of teachers stands outside,
the passion of the lover entered.

> Whenever he read the Sacred Books,
> and something struck his mind
> he imprinted it tenaciously on his memory,
> because he did not grasp in vain
> what his attentive mind heard,
> for he would mull over it
> with affection and constant devotion.[8]

What Bonaventure is getting at in his description of Francis's keen sense of the true meaning of Scripture is that it was not academic study of the texts but the saint's life that allowed him to have clarity in understanding. To put it another way, Francis had become so much a "doer of the word" that his whole life exhibited the fullest understanding of God's revelation.

Bonaventure goes on to explain that Francis's living of Scripture, spurred on by his "unflagging zeal for prayer with a continual exercise of virtue," led the *Poverello*, the little poor man from Assisi, to become a prophet of God. This, it seems by the Franciscan example, is the purpose of all Christian lives— to live Scripture as "doers of the word" and therefore become prophets for our world.

Now, I know what you're thinking: *Does that mean I get to predict the future and do that sort of thing?* No, not really. See, this popular idea of what it means to be a prophet stems from one's ability to see into the future and is not really an authentic Christian notion. If we look back into the scriptural tradition, rarely do we see this contemporary conception of a prophet. Instead we see another type—one who has ability to see the world as it really is. I know, that doesn't sound as *cool* as predicting the future, but think a little bit about the Old Testament prophets. These were members of the Israelite community who looked around and saw the injustice of the world. They cried out against how the powerful were abusing the weak and how the rich were harming the poor. The prophets of Israel looked at the status quo through the eyes of God, from the perspective of Scripture, and said, "This is not right!" Likewise, we see in the New Testament the greatest prophet of the time, John the Baptist, looking at what was happening in his own time and decrying wrongdoing (which ultimately got him beheaded) while also announcing the coming reign of God in the person of Jesus of Nazareth. There were many people who knew Jesus, yet the Gospels tell us that John was really the first to see him for who he really was—the Son of God, the One Who was to come.

The more one lives a life rooted in Scripture, the more one begins to see the world as God sees the world. This leads to some practical implications that arise from an increasingly prophetic lifestyle. One thing is that, in seeing reality truly for what it is, not the glossed-over experience of the everyday that is manufactured or virtual but the holy reality of God's presence in the world, you can no longer continue to live the way you once lived. The good news of the Kingdom of God that Jesus proclaimed calls us to transform our lives from a self-centered to an other-centered way of living (something we'll look at more closely in the next chapter).

The prophetic call of gospel life is not easy and comes at a cost. Part of the cost is the surrender of our own desire and will in exchange for the will of God. Also, living the prophetic call of gospel life may make one unpopular, like the biblical prophets and Francis himself, in a culture and world that does not recognize the value in living for others as God in Christ has lived for us. Instead we live in a world that favors selfish ambition and personal gratification, even at times at the expense of others.

What Scripture does is provide us with an ongoing reminder of who

God is for us so that we might be more and more Godlike or Christlike for others. Like love letters that reveal the intimate relationship shared between two people and that call them to move beyond themselves into a fuller sense of love, Scripture unveils the relationship God has with us. What we are called to do, then, is to let that love story of God and humanity become the story of our lives.

Important Points to Remember
- One way to think of Scripture is as a collection of love letters from God, the story of God's relationship with humanity throughout history.
- God's name reveals and describes who God is: the One who will be there for us and cares deeply about our situations in life.
- Francis of Assisi had such a great love of Scripture and cared so deeply for the Word of God that he insisted that even the smallest pieces of paper that contained a passage from the Bible be treated with reverence and respect.
- The way that Francis allowed the Word of God to speak to his heart, much like the way we might allow the words of a loved one to touch ours, led him into a new way of living. Living the gospel life allows us to become prophets in our world.

Reflection Questions
1. When have I received a "love letter" from someone? How did I feel when I received this expression of love, and how did I respond to it?
2. What examples of love letters have I seen in films and books, on TV and online and in art? Or heard in music? What common threads or ideas are in these expressions of love?
3. How do I understand the story of my relationship with God? Do I see that reflected in Scripture?
4. If I were to write a love letter to God, what would I say?

5. In what ways are God's love letters—Scripture—part of my life? Could I find more time to read and reflect on God's love letters?

chapter seven

Being for Others as God Is for Us

Solidarity and Social Justice

And after the Lord gave me some brothers, no one showed me what I had to do, but the Most High Himself revealed to me that I should live according to the pattern of the Holy Gospel.
—St. Francis[1]

Going in Peace to Serve God and One Another

My friend Julianne has always been involved in the Church. From an early age she shared her musical skills as an accomplished flutist and singer with her parish community and over time became more and more interested in music ministry and the liturgy. She grew up and went off to college to study music and afterward accepted her first job as the director of liturgical music at a parish near Baltimore. The parish was your typical suburban, American Catholic experience. Middle-class and wealthy parishioners filled the seats when this relatively young Christian community would gather each Sunday to celebrate the Eucharist.

Over the course of several years of working there, Julianne came to realize that she needed a change. She took a yearlong job working as a high-school campus minister before deciding to go back to school, this time to study liturgy and theology at the graduate level. At this point, the formerly content young woman, the liturgical novice-turned-expert, began to feel unsettled by the course of her career and engagement with the Church. A question began to arise in her reflection, prayer, and conversation with friends: *What is ministry?*

On the surface, it seemed that Julianne had been doing "ministry" all along. Most people look at those who work for the Church in one capacity or another as de facto ministers and therefore as performing some sort of ministry. But that was precisely the concern. Instead of being something that one embraced with his or her whole life, ministry that is performance or career is not quite the same thing as *ministry* that is lived and life-giving.

It was around this time in her life that I got to know Julianne, a classmate in graduate school who would come to be a good friend of mine. I was one of the people with whom she talked about this question of ministry and *ministry*. See, what she was struggling with was the isolation or, more aptly, the limited experience of ever knowing a community exactly like the one she grew up in, a community that looked exactly like her and her family, a community of affluence and relative comfort. Sure, everybody needs a faith community and therefore everybody deserves dedicated lay and ordained ministers to lead and support parishes for all people. Nevertheless, if ministry was supposed to be something more like service and the example of Jesus Christ in the Gospels, then shouldn't we be with those whom Jesus was with, shouldn't we be looking for where the Spirit guides us, and shouldn't we be more concerned with helping others who need our help than with helping ourselves to a convenient life?

Julianne seemed to think so. What she ultimately came to realize was that her previous decade of experience working in the Church, as blessed as it may have been, was a particularly limited experience. It was sheltered in many ways from the needs of those most desperately in need of her outreach, her talents, and her love. Always a prayerful person dedicated to personal prayer in addition to helping to lead a worshipping community in prayer and song, Julianne understood that the focus of her previous work had been largely about her. Well, it was largely about her and God. The stability and lack of challenge present in her parochial work allowed her to focus her energy on her own wants and needs for God. But that was no longer enough for her. Her personal experience and her studies in the classroom began to expose her to the world outside of her limited experience of "God and me," a world that the Spirit, like Jesus in the desert, was driving her into.

After nearly a decade of work in the Church and graduate studies in liturgy and theology, she decided it was time for her to make a change in her life and start living *ministry*. She made the decision to do something completely different with her life and entered a year of service with the Franciscan Volunteer Ministry in Wilmington, Delaware, working with and living among the poor, abandoned, and voiceless in society. She worked in a women's prison, taught music at an inner-city school, and entered into relationship with people she never would have imagined it possible for her to enter into relationship with. Her world was changed by the embrace of a life of service. Ministry was no longer performed but became a faith that was lived. Her relationship with God, open as it was to the inspiration of the Holy Spirit, could not remain static. Like all relationships, those with God change and call us to move beyond our comfort zones.

From Selfish to Selfless: The Franciscan Story

It is well known that St. Francis had no intention of starting a new religious community, let alone transforming the Church and Christian spirituality in the many ways he would. Francis set out to do his own thing for God. By himself. Alone.

Francis as a young adult, around the age of twenty-four, began to live in a new way. Believing that God was calling him to live a new and radical form of life, one that aligned more closely with the gospel of Jesus Christ, he made some big changes to his lifestyle. Known for what we might today call a partying lifestyle, Francis hung out with his friends from Assisi and enjoyed spending money, celebrating life with his friends, and wearing the latest fashions. He wasn't necessarily a bad guy or more sinful than any typical American young adult today, relatively speaking. Had Francis been born in 1985, we might imagine him to be your all-around college nice guy, who enjoyed frat parties and socializing but also went to church on Sunday. Not so bad.

However, in his early twenties he began to become restless with the way his life was going. A series of events recorded some years later help to explain the experience Francis had in what we now understand to be the beginning of his conversion. He felt that God was asking him to change his life, to move beyond himself and the superficial lifestyle he had been living all along, and to redirect his focus to God and Christ's church. This experience is depicted in the often told story of the crucifix at the chapel of San Damiano. The crucifix spoke to Francis, saying, "Francis, rebuild my church."

Another event that became a transformative for the future saint was his experience of the leper. At the end of his life, St. Francis still vividly recalled how his life was dramatically changed by the encounter of his marginalized brother. In his *Testament*, that collection of thoughts that Francis, on his deathbed, dictated to his brother friars, the dying saint from Assisi began:

> The Lord gave me, Brother Francis, thus to begin doing penance in this way: for when I was in sin, it seemed too bitter for me to see lepers. And the Lord Himself led me among them and *I*

showed mercy to them. And when I left them, what had seemed
bitter to me was turned into sweetness of soul and body. And
afterwards I delayed a little and left the world.[2]

His biographers explain that something happened during that first
experience when Francis moved beyond his fears of those who were
different, unwanted and poor. The leper was for Francis what so many
forgotten or abandoned people are for us today: the homeless veteran,
the HIV/AIDS victim, the practitioner of another religious tradition,
the immigrant, or the outcast. The ability of Francis to look at the leper
and see the face of a human being, his brother, and not an object to be
dismissed and despised—that is what so powerfully changed Francis's
life.

These two key moments, experiencing the grace of Christ's call to
more intentionally follow the gospel and embracing the previously
unembraceable, led Francis to realize that there was no going back to
the way he used to live. He had to change.

The way he changed his life was to go off on his own and literally
rebuild an old country church that had fallen into ruin outside the
city of Assisi. Taking what he understood to be Jesus's call to "rebuild
his church," the young man from Assisi sought to live up to these new
expectations and life mission in the most complete way, so he lived at
the church and spent his days in prayer while reconstructing the site
brick by brick. His curious new way of living—going from playboy to
recluse—caught the attention of many in his hometown. Rumors began
to circulate about what this "crazy" Francis was really up to, and some
folks had to come and see for themselves.

What happened next was something that Francis did not plan for,
and probably couldn't. Some of those who saw his new way of life, the
changes Francis adopted, became inspired. They, too, wanted to live a

life untethered by the frivolities of the day, the concerns about acquiring more and more wealth, serving their own desires. They saw the budding of a special joy in the heart of Francis, and they wanted to experience that too. These folks started hanging around Francis, helping him with his rebuilding project, discussing the new changes with him and sharing their faith with one another.

It became increasingly clear, especially as more and more young men (and later young women following Clare of Assisi) traveled out of the city to hang around Francis in the countryside, that God's plan was not the same as Francis's plan. Francis had intended only to live a life of penance, service, and prayer on his own, just him and God. Yet, the Christian life—as Francis quickly learned—cannot be about just an individual and God. Christianity, which is following the gospel life, is about community and solidarity, it is about prayer and service.

From Religious Isolation to Christian Solidarity

Both the modern story of my friend Julianne and the classic narrative of Francis of Assisi offer us insight into the way we are called to live the gospel life today. Although each person's life has its own share of challenges and circumstances, we are all called to transcend the limitations of a self-centered focus on religion and embrace a life of Christian solidarity after the example of God in Jesus Christ. How we do that specifically may vary, but collectively we can look to the Franciscan tradition for guidance in growing in faith, which ultimately leads to service, community, and solidarity.

Today's world can be very isolating. It's curious that the advances in technology and communication that allow us to remain connected to one another at all times of the day or night and in all parts of the world also seem to prohibit us from engaging with one another in the rich and meaningful ways necessary to sustain intimate relationships.

This is particularly challenging for young adults—although it is also a concern for people of all ages in a digitally saturated world—who have a strong desire to be a part of a community. Yet, in a unique way, today's young adults have grown up in a time of increasing global consciousness, easily accessible travel, and near-instant communication. The hyper-connectedness of technology, however, leaves many young adults seeking something more.

While people today have access to the mundane details of others' daily activities, thoughts, and plans, the ways in which human beings connect have drastically changed. We are more like isolated Lone Rangers who interact with one another through the veil of technology, remaining always a "virtual arm's length" away. The illusion of a more community-centered experience of the global family has really, in many ways, helped usher in a more individualistic culture. It is also a technological culture that promotes passivity in relationship, allowing for individuals to log in to see the experiences and views of another from afar without the burden or reciprocity that comes with a more authentic experience of relationship. In other words, I have no obligation to you or anyone else, I am simply a consumer of information—it just happens to be information about your life.

There is a tendency for this increasingly omnipresent culture to bleed into our spiritual and prayer lives. While there has always been a danger of letting our faith become just about "God and me," something that all Christians must struggle to avoid, citizens of today's world face an even greater challenge as the way most people enter into and maintain relationships shifts. It might be more difficult for us to break out of what Francis experienced early in his life while striving to live the gospel alone. He had the advantage—although I doubt he saw it that way at first—of people coming out to where he was and engaging him.

In ways, I am sure, that forced him to face the fuller call of the gospel and to be an active member of the community in working with and for others in following the example of Christ. Today we have to be more conscious of how we go about interacting with others in our effort to live out a more gospel-centered life.

The bottom line is that we can't live a Christian life alone. Likewise, we cannot live a Christian life under the guise of exclusively superficial and virtual relationships. We must live as active and engaged members of the community of believers, what we call the Body of Christ, which is just a theologically fancy way of saying "the Church." But how do we do this?

Action, Lifestyle, and Power in Christian Conversion

One way to recognize the "signs of the times," as the Second Vatican Council described it, is to see what is needed from us to better serve the global human family. Part of recognizing those signs should result in joining with the rest of creation to celebrate the joys and blessings of life. We need to remember that who we are as created by God is inherently good, as is all of creation, and therefore we should recall our goodness and live in the world optimistically in light of Christian hope. But there is also a need in our time to identify the injustice and evil that is to be expected in a finite and imperfect world. How we respond to that type of need reveals much about how we live the Christian life.

The Gospels are filled with examples of Jesus responding to the needs of God's people. He does this primarily through teaching and healing, although sometimes his simple presence is enough. Those who are troubled mentally, spiritually, and physically come to him so that they might find healing in the love of God. How many people like that come and go in our own lives? How well do we respond to their needs? If we dare to bear the name "Christian," then we should strive to live that responsibility to the best of our ability.

This is what Francis wanted to do. At first, as we've already seen, Francis thought that what he needed to do to be a good Christian was to live simply by himself, spending lots of time in private prayer and working (quite literally) in a church. This is not an uncommon starting point for many people seeking to live a fuller Christian life even today. Perhaps such a journey begins with forgoing some behaviors or attitudes that previously separated you from God. Maybe it begins with more time set aside for prayer or greater involvement in the Church. It is possible that such inspiration to live a fuller Christian life leads some to a form of service in the community.

In a way, these examples demonstrate concrete actions in the life of a Christian and are, in part at least, essential elements of what it means to live the gospel in the world. We can call this the beginning of one's lifelong or ongoing conversion toward becoming more and more Christlike. For Francis it began with the work he did in the little chapel of San Damiano, seeking to "rebuild the church" as he felt called by Jesus Christ to do. For my friend Julianne and others, it began with a desire to participate more fully in Church ministries that draw us closer to the mysteries that we celebrate. For you it may begin in any number of ways.

Yet, like Francis, Julianne, and countless other Christians, we cannot stay in the realm of concrete actions. While our whole life should reflect a commitment to what we commonly call service and ministry, we must also allow for God's Spirit to work in our lives as in the case of Francis. The famous South American theologian Gustavo Gutiérrez has said that authentic Christian conversion happens in three identifiable phases. Each of these phases might look different for each person as one examines the details and there is no set, one-size-fits-all time frame that can easily describe this process or its parts. The first phase is that of concrete actions that we've talked about already. This is a conscious effort on the part of a person to *do something* different in response to the call of the gospel: praying more, going to church, reading Scripture (love letters from God!), serving at a soup kitchen, and so on. Thomas of Celano, Francis's first biographer, remembers that Francis first began to change his attitude and only later started to act in accordance with his new outlook. That was what led to the saint's engagement in concrete actions and was his initial commitment to follow God's will in dedicated ways.

The next way one responds to God's invitation to conversion happens in the willing and conscious shift of one's lifestyle. What Gutiérrez observes is that as one becomes more and more committed to the concrete actions of Christian living, it will necessarily follow that he or she will come to see that there are ways in which his or her lifestyle could better reflect the gospel life. This is a powerful yet difficult aspect of Christian living for people today, especially in places like the United States, where so many are so fortunate to have so much. What's more is that the culture in places like America promotes a sense of insatiability for more and more things, the latest this or that, and the most luxurious or expensive products. Nice things in themselves are not bad, but the challenge of gospel life is to focus on the things that God values and not the passing things that a consumer culture and an advertising industry value. For Francis this change in lifestyle happened gradually, as I believe it does in the experience of conversion for most people. These sorts of things don't happen overnight.

For Francis, doing charitable works quickly came to lead the young man to examine how he lived his everyday life. It would no longer work for Francis to proverbially "helicopter in" from his comfortable lifestyle in the city of Assisi, even if what he was doing was charitable work—that is, selling his (and, at times, his family's) things to give money to the poor, donating his knight's armor to an unfortunate noble, and rebuilding a dilapidated church. There came a point when Francis decided that he had to take an additional step, he had to shift his lifestyle from one of relative comfort to one that honored the Christian call to protest the disparity in what the wealthy had and what the poor and outcast lacked. It is at this point that Francis began to seek refuge in the very churches he was repairing, his first attempt at the experiment that would later be called the Franciscan Order, whose members sought to live *sine proprio*—without anything of one's own. He would rely on the generosity of God and strive to give all he could to those who had even less.

If you could afford to buy this book, chances are that you live a lifestyle that could use some evaluation (not that purchasing this book is a bad thing, don't get me wrong). I am a professed Franciscan friar and I continually have to reevaluate the way I live my life, as do all those who are serious about authentic gospel living. Those who have disposable incomes, the latest technologies, and the nicest homes, cars, clothing, and the like are the ones most in need of examining a lifestyle that sets one above and apart from others.

Francis is remembered to have said that one of the reasons the friars were to own no possessions is that then they could be free to use their lives and energy for good things in the world. The more we have, the more concerned we are about acquiring the newest and best things and the more energy we expend protecting our property and securing our finances. In a world where nearly a quarter of the earth's population is in poverty, for those who have so much there arises the challenge to examine what can be done about the imbalance of wealth. But so much of our contemporary culture is geared to distracting us from that examination of lifestyle. How we live, how we spend our money, what we do with the things entrusted to us are not distinct from who we are as Christians. They really stand close to the center of what we are about.

The last phase of this invitation to Christian conversion follows closely from the reexamination and adjustment of one's lifestyle. After Francis began to live a new way of life, selling what he had to give to the poor and living on the generosity of others in the Church, he made a decisive and final break with his social class. The biographies of the saint present the scene when, before the bishop of Assisi in the town square, Francis renounces his father and the stability, status, and inheritance associated with his family. No longer was Francis somewhere in the realm of the merchant class, the privileged pseudo-nobility of Assisi, but now he was intentionally moving to the place of the *minores*, or lesser ones, who were often outcast or dismissed. While this break with his social class certainly signaled a lifestyle change that clearly affirmed the path Francis had chosen by his earlier actions, more important was that Francis declared that his stance would be one of refusing power in this world. The adage is somewhat true: Money is power. In this case, Francis's total rejection of money and, even more so, of his social-class affiliations was a sign of stepping out from the power games of the day.

This was the vision, basic as it was in the early days, that Francis had of what his way of life should be about. To follow Christ was to follow in the humility of God's own powerlessness exemplified in the Incarnation (becoming a completely dependent human being) and the cross (being crucified as a criminal). For what appears to be foolishness to the world, as St. Paul tells us and as Francis lived, is God's wisdom in which God's weakness is more powerful than human strength (1 Corinthians 1:25). The French medieval historian Jacques Dalarun explains:

In its beginnings, the Order that is called "Franciscan," or more accurately "The Order of Friars Minor," was a fraternity of mostly lay individuals who decided to do penance. The founder, in his concern to live "according to the form of the Holy Gospel," chose to establish in a rule of religious life the condition shared by the most powerless classes in the society of his time: destitution, precariousness, itinerancy, manual labor. He showed a loathing for all forms of power that went far beyond the scorn of this world as found in the monastic and ascetic tradition. With Francis, there is less of a merely visible break with the world; at the heart of his life there is instead more intransigence toward any compromise with the world and its powers.[3]

When Francis publicly broke with his social class, he made a statement to the world about what it meant to him to follow in the footprints of Christ in the pattern of the gospel. His desire was not simply to serve the poor and marginalized, not only to adjust his lifestyle to better reflect his Christian values, but to renounce the world's power so as to be in solidarity with the powerless, the voiceless, and the forgotten in society.

People exert so much energy today to ignore the powerless, striving in their own lives to acquire as much power as possible in the form of influence, money, status, and class. Such an effort is made to affirm the "value" and "importance" of consumerism and individual achievement. As a result, those who, largely owing to no responsibility of their own, live in poverty often become the scorn of the affluent and blamed for their own circumstances. More and more often this has become the cultural attitude of our time, it reflects the "wisdom" of the powerful who desire to maintain the status quo at all costs. Yet Francis recognized that the wisdom of God, demonstrated both in God becoming human in the case of Jesus Christ and in the scriptural narratives that time and again place God on the side of the poor and marginalized, demands something radical on our part. This radical break with the values of the world is difficult, and something that many are not willing to attempt. Nevertheless, it is the goal and aim of the Franciscan tradition of spirituality in this world.

How can we ever be expected to live that way? I'm not sure that we are, at least I'm not convinced that Francis's personal journey, in scope and detail, is the path for every Christian. I don't think that he would have expected as much. However, we are *all called* to live a life of Christian conversion, which means that the path from selfishness to selflessness is what is expected of all the baptized. If we wish to follow after the example of Francis, then our lives, while perhaps not as luminous as Francis's was, should reflect the gospel in our actions, in our lifestyle, and in our refusal of power, which positions us in a place of solidarity with the powerless, marginalized, and poor of our world.

Important Points to Remember
- Our prayer lives, our relationships with God, cannot be limited to just "me and God" but should overflow to be a live-giving source of service to the whole human family.
- Francis in his youth was not necessarily a bad guy or sinful person any more than the typical young adult of our own day, but he came to realize that to be a disciple of Christ and to live the gospel required that he make some significant changes to his life.
- While seeking to live his new life alone, Francis eventually came to realize that Christian discipleship is about community and not individuality.
- We should not let the increasingly individualistic and isolating culture bleed over into our spiritual and prayer lives but strive instead to be in

solidarity with all of our sisters and brothers according to the gospel.

• We can start with concrete and charitable actions but need to shift our lifestyles and break with cultural ties that inhibit living the Christian life. Ultimately, we should strive to reflect the gospel in our actions, in our lifestyle, and in our refusal of power.

Reflection Questions

1. Am I concerned with helping others, in making my family, my workplace, my community a better place to live? How do I help on a practical level?

2. When I think about helping others, what am I willing to do? What takes me out of my comfort zone? What steps do I need to take to move out of this comfort zone?

3. Whom do I consider to be someone who is "rebuilding"—rebuilding family, community, church, nation, world? What can I do to rebuild?

4. How can I reflect in my own life the three-stage model of conversion in Francis's life? Where am I in the process right now? What do I need to do to reach the next stage?

5. In what ways am I isolated from the world? Is this isolation self-imposed, of my own making? Why do I seek this isolation? What could/should I do to break out of a "me-centered" world and break into a gospel-centered life?

chapter eight

"Praise Be You, Lord, Through Brother Sun"
Creation

Most High, all-powerful, good Lord,
Yours are *the praises, the glory*, and *the honor*, and all *blessing*,
To You alone, Most High, do they belong,
and no human is worthy to mention Your name.
—St. Francis[1]

Taking a Look at the Whole Family

This book is about relationship, which shouldn't come as a surprise at this point, because the core of Franciscan life is precisely the reality of relationship. It is the experience of God who loves each of us into creation and remains with us always, even when we feel distant from that love. It is the experience of others with whom we have been born into relationship, a reality made even more striking in God's decision to enter the world as a member of the human family. Yet the significance of relationship in the Franciscan tradition doesn't end with a universal sense of connectedness with the rest of humanity. In fact, what St. Francis of Assisi is perhaps best known for is his radical inclusion of *all of creation* in his spirituality of relationship with God. Human beings are not above and against or better than the rest of creation but part of creation, as one might be part of a very large family. That's why Francis called all aspects of God's creation his brothers and sisters.

Using an early document of the Franciscan tradition called *The Assisi Compilation*, a collection of remembrances of the saint's life by those who knew him, Thomas Murtagh describes Francis's particular love of all aspects of creation:

> Next to fire he had an especial love for water, because it symbolizes holy penitence and tribulation, and at Baptism the soul is cleansed from its stains and receives its first purification. So whenever he washed his hands he chose a place where the water would not be trodden underfoot as it fell to the ground. For the same reason, whenever he had to walk over rocks, he trod reverently and fearfully, out of love for Christ Who is called The Rock: so whenever he recited the psalm Thou wilt set me high upon a rock, he used to say with great reverence and devotion, "Thou hast set me up at the foot of the rock."
>
> He told the friar who cut and chopped the wood for the fire that he must never cut down the whole tree, but remove branches in such a way that part of the tree remained intact, out of love for Christ, Who willed to accomplish our salvation on the wood of the cross.
>
> In the same way he told the friar who cared for the gardens not to cultivate all the ground for vegetables, but to set aside a plot to grow flowers to bloom in their season, out of love for Him Who is called The Rose on the plain and the lily on the mountain slopes. Indeed, he told the brother-gardener that he should always make a pleasant flower-garden, and cultivate every variety of fragrant herb and flowering plant, so that all who saw the herbs and flowers would be moved to praise God.[2]

The way in which Francis is described in this passage might suggest to some readers that Francis was a bit crazy or at least foolish, but that is precisely what the saint from Assisi would have expected—maybe even what he would have desired! Francis is remembered to have appropriated the title "God's fool" (*idiota* in Latin) in order to live up to what St. Paul in his letters teaches when it comes to the wisdom of God appearing as foolishness to the world.

In a way, care for creation, let alone recognizing all elements of creation as part of one large family, seems like foolishness. This is particularly true in an age that is so focused on individual success and achievement at the expense of others that thinking about nonhuman parts of creation seems like a big waste of time, unless of course it might benefit me in some way. Francis, by contrast, had absolutely nothing to gain by being God's fool, by loving creation for what it is, as God loves all of creation for just that reason. I really don't think that Francis cared all that much about what others thought of him, a disposition that is difficult to cultivate today in a world that is so concerned about image and appearance. Yet the model of care for creation that the Franciscan tradition offers us challenges us to move away from our convenience and self-interest to be a little foolish for the sake of the earth, which indeed is more than a playground for our use.

Humanity's Playground or God's House?

I always love teaching the doctrine of creation to college students. At Siena College, a small Catholic Franciscan liberal-arts college near Albany, New York, I've taught a course that offers an overview of Christian systematic theology. Each section of the course relates to one of the major subsections of the academic study of theology—to themes such as revelation, Christology, and ecclesiology. We aren't able to delve too deeply into any one of them—a real shame for a theology nerd like me, but perhaps a relief for the students who can be at times a bit less excited about systematic theology than I usually am.

When we discuss the doctrine of creation, I begin by drawing a line on the board with the terms "Humanity's playground" on one side and "God's house" on the other. At that point I ask the students where we might mark the spot on that continuum where the Christian tradition would identify the doctrine of creation. In other words, how should Christians understand creation? Inevitably students will start raising hands and offering a location on the line. I always press them a little for the reason they select this or that location nearer or farther from one side or the other. I get all sorts of answers from the stereotypical college shrug ("I dunno") to well-thought-out responses that reflect some deeper consideration of the subject.

Usually at this point in the semester, long after I have delivered the introductory lectures on the purpose, sources, and methods of theology, I expect the students to respond to the following question instantly: *What is the normative source for Christian theology that we must always consider alongside all other sources?* The answer: Scripture. My next question: *What does* Scripture *say about where we should plot along the line?* It is here that the students usually get a little quiet, unsure of how to respond.

It is then that I offer a theological translation of the two foci of the line from "humanity's playground" to "God's house." I explain that one end is another way of naming the "dominion" model of creation that has been popular throughout the centuries, while the other end is something a little less known, something called the "kinship" model. The dominion model suggests that all aspects of creation were brought into existence by God to serve the needs and, at times, the whims of humankind. It is this outlook that has been invoked through the years to justify human practices and industries that wreak havoc on the environment: oil drilling, mining, deforestation, industrial agriculture, draining lakes, and so on. On the other hand, the kinship model of creation sees all of creation as always and already in relationship with all of humankind. Men and women are *part of* and not *above* the rest of creation.

Scripture, on closer examination, supports this latter model. We see in the Genesis accounts of creation that God's Spirit was already at work in the cosmos, breathing the same life that would form humanity's first breath into the chaos of the world. Plants, animals, and all the elements share in the glory of being part of God's creation, albeit in a different way from that in which human beings do. Men and women are given the unique and special gift of being able to enter into relationship. We can choose to be in relationship with God—with others *and* with the rest of creation.

Our obligation to care for the rest of creation, then, does not stem from our being given dominion or stewardship over the world as if we were masters or landlords of earth. Instead, it arises from our responsibility to tend to the needs of the cosmos, to protect all life and regard all aspects of God's creation as individually loved into existence by God.

I like to tell my college students that the difference is like that between what is entrusted to their care (something like their on-campus student apartments) and something that has been passed on to them that they have a family connection to and perhaps own (like their parents' or grandparents' house). On reflection, the students confess that there is indeed a distinction in their own attitude toward the two objects in each situation. The students, rather casually, admit that they feel less compelled to "take care" of something that was not "theirs." The evidence is not simply hypothetical but empirically rooted in the statistical reports that colleges and universities generate every year, reports that account for the destruction of property on campus and the subsequent repair and replacement costs.

Creation, Scripture reveals, is like the home that is very much a part of our family. We live in it, it is an honor to do so, but our connection to it is more than that of a temporary keeper or overseer. We belong to a cosmic family tied together by God's loving act of creation. We may be different from squirrels, trees, and rocks, but we are part of the same act of Divine Love.

Francis knew this intuitively. Without taking a university course in systematic theology, he was able to read the Word of God in Scripture and in the natural world around him and see the manifold ways he was tied to each aspect of the world. His explicit choice to call each aspect of creation his brother or sister bespeaks the ultimate reality of which the saint from Assisi was so intimately aware. In addition to texts like *The Assisi Compilation* and the many biographies written about Francis after his death, Francis himself penned a canticle that reveals this spiritual insight. What has come to be known as Francis's *Canticle of the Creatures* is perhaps his most famous piece of writing.

Most High, all-powerful, good Lord,
    Yours are *the praises, the glory,* and *the honor,* and all *blessing,*
To You alone, Most High, do they belong,
    and no human is worthy to mention Your name.
Praised be You, my *Lord,* with all *Your creatures,*
    especially Sir Brother Sun,
Who is the day and through whom You give us light.
And he is beautiful and radiant with great splendor;
    and bears a likeness of You, Most High One.
Praised be You, my Lord, through Sister *Moon* and the *stars,*
    in heaven You formed them clear and precious and beautiful.
Praised be You, my Lord, through Brother Wind,
    and through the air, cloudy and serene, and every kind of weather,
through whom You give sustenance to Your creatures.

Praised be You, my Lord, through Sister *Water*,
who is very useful and humble and precious and chaste.
Praised be You, my Lord, through Brother *Fire*,
through whom *You light the night*,
and he is beautiful and playful and robust and strong.
Praised be You, my Lord, through our Sister Mother *Earth*,
who sustains and governs us,
and who produces various *fruit* with colored flowers and *herbs*.
Praised be You, my Lord, through those who give pardon for Your love,
and bear infirmity and tribulation.
Blessed are those who endure in peace
for by You, Most High, shall they be crowned.
Praised be You, my Lord, through our Sister Bodily Death,
from whom no one living can escape.
Woe to those who die in mortal sin.
Blessed are those whom death will find in Your most holy will,
for *the second death* shall do them no harm.
Praise and *bless* my *Lord* and give Him thanks
and serve Him with great humility.[3]

Franciscan spirituality reflects the notion of a kinship model of creation, for Francis was not concerned about how this or that element of creation could be harnessed and controlled by humankind for its benefits but instead saw in admiration the gift that each part of the created order was in the eyes of God.

Relating to Creation Today

Today, perhaps more than ever, we need the kinship outlook on creation that the Franciscan tradition has always espoused. As we face ecological crises on many fronts, the previously adopted model of dominion has proven to be not only wrongheaded but also sinful. What the Franciscan tradition offers people today is a language, a mind-set, an approach to the rest of creation that reflects a love for and solidarity with the rest of the created order and that draws us into an ever deeper relationship with God. To remember that we are part of creation is to remember, in part, from where we—and all creation—originated.

The theologian Sr. Elizabeth Johnson, C.S.J., has written a lot about the need we have as a Christian community to reconsider the overwhelmingly popular dominion approach to creation and replace it with something more like the Franciscan kinship model. One of the most powerful ways she illustrates our human and nonhuman interconnectedness within creation, focusing in a unique way on what it means to be part of the very same cosmic reality of God's love, is her description of human beings as made of "space dust."

She explains that our interconnectedness is as biological as it is theological.[4] The air we breathe, the iron in our blood, the calcium in our bones, all of who we are materially is part of and originated out of some other part of God's creation. Perhaps some Christians would prefer to ignore the theological reasons for why we need to refocus our attention on the kinship we humans share with the rest of creation, but Johnson points out that we cannot ignore the scientific interconnections. The elements, the atoms, the quanta that make up our world make us who we are too, further reflecting that truth that Francis and his followers recognized in their own lives: All of creation is part of the same cosmic family.

We see signs of the kinship of all creation throughout Scripture too. We find God's creation intimately connected to the actions of human suffering, flourishing, and sinfulness such as what we read in the book of the prophet Hosea:

Swearing, lying, and murder,
   and stealing and adultery break out;
   bloodshed follows bloodshed.
Therefore the land mourns,
   and all who live in it languish;
together with the wild animals and the birds of the air,
   even the fish of the sea are perishing. (4:2–3)

We read in the book of Job about how God cares for and sustains *all* creation, including humanity, a truth that the protagonist Job struggles to accept (Job 12:7–10). We pray the Hebrew prayers of the Psalms, which time and again recall the familial relationship the rest of creation shares with humanity as God's beloved creation (see, for example, Psalms 65, 135, 145, 147, 148, and others).

And in the New Testament we read some of the most compelling scriptural articulations of the kinship of creation in the writings of St. Paul. Take this example from Paul's letter to the Romans:

> For the creation was subjected to futility, not of its own will but by the will of the one who subjected it, in hope that the creation itself would be set free from the bondage to decay and will obtain the freedom of the glory of the children of God. We know that the whole creation has been groaning in labor pains until now; and not only the creation, but we ourselves, who have the first fruits of the Spirit, groan inwardly while we wait for adoption, the redemption of our bodies. (Romans 8:20–23).

What Francis saw in the world around him was precisely what St. Paul wrote about to the Romans more than a millennium earlier. Salvation is not just about human beings going to heaven or getting the first-class treatment while the rest of creation is stuck in coach. All of creation eagerly awaits the return back to God because all of creation is united in kinship.

It would seem that science and theology, Scripture and experience point us in a direction that challenges us to transform the way we see the world. As we come to see God, ourselves, one another, and creation as Francis and his followers did, we should come to see that all of these seemingly different connections are joined together in a harmony of love that finds its origin in God. As human beings we have been given a special role in creation. We have been created *imago Dei*—in the image and likeness of God. This means that we have the freedom to enter or refuse relationship. While it seems obvious and insignificant at first— "yeah, tell me something I don't know"—the truth is that it is up to us to live in such a way that we reflect our vocation with the ability to be in relationship.

Francis, Clare, and the men and women who followed them through the centuries were in part drawn to their ways of life because of the inclusive and relational quality of their example. Why is Francis depicted so frequently with animals in forests or near water? Perhaps it has something to do with the recognition that Francis models right relationship between humanity and creation. Just as we can think of good models of how to be in relationship with family members or friends, Francis's life, writings, and example provide a model for how to be in right relationship with *all* creation, which necessarily includes others and ourselves. Yet, this model of right relationship also includes God at the center.

In their popular book on Franciscan environmental spirituality, *Care for Creation: A Franciscan Spirituality of the Earth*, Ilia Delio, Keith Douglass Warner, o.f.m., and Pamela Wood remind us that creation was never "humanity's playground" for Francis: "Francis taught the brothers to accept the gifts of God's goodness in creation and to respond with grateful hearts through bonds of love, care, concern and companionship. Francis valued the home of the earth not as *his* home alone but first and foremost as *God's* home."[5] When Francis looked around the world, when he saw another person, when he thought of himself, what he saw were these things in relationship to God. God was the source and it was God's love and goodness that produced *everything*.

A few decades after Francis's death, the Franciscan minister general, St. Bonaventure, would describe creation as bearing the footprints of God. Everything, Bonaventure asserted, reflects the Creator. One is able to see in each tiny or grand aspect of the world around us the indelible mark of God, the one who loved everything into being. In this way, the world is seen as belonging to God, but it does not belong to God in the way that your car or any other type of property might belong to you. All of creation belongs to God as this or that trait in a child belongs to his or her parents, or as a piece of art belongs to an artist. God is present in creation as a reflection or image or footprint of the one who brought it lovingly into existence.

How then can we relate to this creation? How is it that we are expected to live differently in light of this truth? What is asked of us?

These are the sorts of questions that we need to continually ask ourselves. We can begin by following the Franciscan model of relationship with all of creation. We can recognize the sensitive network of life that encompasses the whole cosmos. We can start to see the way we interact, take for granted, or ignore the rest of creation, with which we share our delicate ecosystem. We can work on becoming more aware of how our decisions, our actions, and the way we think about our world might affect the rest of the family of creation in negative or harmful ways.

What is asked of us is simply to be who it is that God created us to be. It is when we try to be something else, something more than a member of the family of creation, that we cause harm to the natural world. I recently watched a documentary in which a scientist said that it is curious that of all the life forms on our planet—trees, whales, birds, dogs—humans are the only creatures that take more resources than they need. Even the big redwoods take from the soil only enough nutrients to grow. Lions kill only one gazelle at a time. Yet human beings have historically taken more and more and more.

Perhaps one way to begin responding to what is asked of us by God is to take an honest look at the way we use and abuse natural resources. How do we use fossil fuels and energy that might harm the environment? How much clean water do we waste each day in the shower, through the faucet, elsewhere? How do we use food, and do we let food go to waste? Is there another way?

It is with little steps, small changes, and a new awareness that we can come to live out what it is that we believe. Francis models this way of life for us, and it is a life of humility in relationship. What the Franciscan tradition reminds us of is our interconnectivity. That just as God is already always in relationship with all of creation, we too, by virtue of being created in God's image and likeness, have the chance to respond to that relationship that is already there and that we so often overlook. Relationships are not meant to be kept hidden, separate from the rest of the world, but oriented outward to include others in service, friendship, and love. A healthy relationship leads toward a better awareness of our interconnectivity and, as Francis shows us, this includes our care of creation.

Important Points to Remember

• Our relationship with God not only extends to our need to be in solidarity and to work for justice and peace among the human family but should also lead us to see our radical interconnectedness with all of creation.

- Francis intuitively realized that we belong to a cosmic family tied together by God's loving act of creation.
- Today, amid the ecological crises our planet faces, we need to return to the kinship model of creation that Francis advocated and lived. This notion of the kinship of all creation is found throughout Scripture.
- We need to translate this view of creation into concrete action by examining how we use natural resources, how our political and social action affects the earth, and how we might work at the local level to bring about positive ecological change in our communities and the world.

Reflection Questions

1. How do I view creation—with a "dominion model" or with a "kinship model"? What signs of either model do I see in the way I think about creation and how I see others treating creation?
2. Do I consider creation part of my cosmic family? Does God? How do I understand the claim in the book of Genesis that, at the end of creating, God said it was very good?
3. How do I harm creation? How do I respect it and reverence it? How do I care for creation? Do I need to live differently? What steps do I need to take to be more aware of earthly resources?
4. In what ways do I see God in creation?

conclusion

✳

LIVING A LIFE OF RELATIONSHIP WITH GOD

Now the word of the LORD came to me saying,
"Before I formed you in the womb I knew you,
and before you were born I consecrated you;
I appointed you a prophet to the nations."
Then I said, "Ah, Lord GOD! Truly I do not know how to speak,
for I am only a boy." But the LORD said to me,
"Do not say, 'I am only a boy';
for you shall go to all to whom I send you,
and you shall speak whatever I command you.
Do not be afraid of them, for I am with you to deliver you,
says the LORD."
—Jeremiah 1:4–8

In the beginning of his book *Already There: Letting God Find You*, Mark Mossa, S.J., writes: "Thus, to speak about a spirituality for young adults is to speak about a spirituality of desire. The goal of that spirituality is nothing more—and nothing less—than to be with God."[6]

Spirituality, especially one that draws on the richness of the Franciscan tradition, has to be about desire. Returning to the starting point of this book: Sitting in that room in New York and reflecting on the writings and legacy of Francis and Clare of Assisi, I believe that the image of dating helps sum up what it means to talk about desire for God. To talk about desire for God is to talk about the "longing and pining" for God (as Psalm 42 puts it) that shines through eight hundred years of tradition and continues to inspire women and men of goodwill today. To talk about Franciscan spirituality for the next generation is to talk about desire, love, and relationship.

There are many ways to live one's life. The blessing and curse of being created in the image and likeness of God is that we get to decide for ourselves which path to take on our earthly pilgrimage. We might start off like the young adult Francis of Assisi, not very concerned about the issues of the world apart from having a good time and making some money. But we might also find ourselves, like Francis a little while later, newly aware of the presence of God in our lives. That presence that draws us forward and calls us to respond to the invitation of relationship that God offers us even before we were born. *"Before I formed you in the womb I knew you, and before you were born I consecrated you; I appointed you a prophet to the nations."*

What has our journey looked like so far? How do we imagine it looking in the future? That we are on a journey of life—a pilgrimage—toward a goal of returning with all of creation to God should open our eyes to see the world anew and to recognize how the love of God, God's desire to be in relationship with us, can change our lives forever. With that new way of seeing the world I don't see my enemy as an enemy but as my brother or sister in Christ. With that new way of seeing the world I don't see creation as an opportunity to exploit or a resource to squander but as a part of the broader cosmic family that God also loves deeply and deliberately chose to create. With that new way of seeing the world I see myself not as something less than or greater than who I am in the sight of God but as my True Self. A Franciscan spirituality for the next generation is about seeing the world as God sees it.

One way the Franciscan tradition should shape or influence our lives is to remind us that our relationship with God is not all that different from our other forms of relationship. It takes communication, time, effort, attention, and love. To be in relationship with God means traveling on the two-way street of shared experience, opening ourselves up to God in a way that allows God into our lives. Perhaps most important, relationship with God means that we can't simply live in isolation ("me and God") to the exclusion of others. The love we share with God should spill over into our interactions with all people, building others up and announcing the Kingdom of God with our lives.

Francis did some amazing things during his life, but it wasn't the extraordinary things that made him a saint and still revered today. Most of Francis's life was lived simply and ordinarily. *How* he did those ordinary things, the embrace of a marginalized person outside the Assisi walls, the conversation with a leader of another faith, the nonviolent being-in-the-world, the love of all creation, the simplicity of his needs and desires—this is what made him a saint. The way we live our lives, striving to make our whole lives our prayer, is what will make us saints too. Our lives of gospel living, our living the Franciscan tradition in the world, deeply in love with God, begins as so many amazing love stories do: with a first date.

notes

❋

Introduction: *Prayer and Relationship*

1. Francis of Assisi, "A Letter to the Entire Order," vv. 28–29, in *The Saint,* vol. 1 of *Francis of Assisi: Early Documents,* ed. Regis Armstrong, J.A. Wayne Hellmann, and William Short (New York: New City, 1999), p. 118. Hereafter referred to as *FA:ED* and followed by volume and page number.
2. See Regis Armstrong and Ingrid Peterson, introduction to *The Franciscan Tradition* (Collegeville, Md.: Liturgical, 2010), pp. xi–xv.
3. Ilia Delio, *Franciscan Prayer* (Cincinnati: St. Anthony Messenger Press, 2004), p. 19.
4. Murray Bodo, *Landscape of Prayer* (Cincinnati: St. Anthony Messenger Press, 2003), p. 3.
5. Francis of Assisi, "The Testament," in *FA:ED* I, p. 124.

Chapter One: *The First Date: The Pilgrimage Begins*

1. Thomas Merton, *No Man Is an Island* (New York: Harcourt Brace, 1955), p. 131.
2. Thomas of Celano, *The Remembrance of the Desire of a Soul,* bk. 2, chap. 163, v. 215, in *FA:ED* II, p. 386.
3. *Gaudium et Spes,* the Pastoral Constitution on the Church in the World, 1.
4. Kathy Matheson, "Google CEO Urges Grads: 'Turn Off Your Computer,'" Associated Press, May 18, 2009.

Chapter Two: *What We Are Before God: The True Self*

1. Bonaventure, *Soliloquium* 1.5, in vol. 3 of The *Works of Bonaventure: Cardinal, Seraphic Doctor, and Saint,* trans. José de Vinck (Paterson, N.J.: St. Anthony Guild, 1966), p. 44. Bonaventure is paraphrasing St.

Augustine's *Confessions* 3.6.11, where Augustine reflects on the proximity of God to us.

2. Thomas Merton, *New Seeds of Contemplation* (New York: New Directions, 1961), p. 34.

3. Francis of Assisi, "Admonition XIX," *FA:ED* II, p. 135.

4. Bonaventure, *On the Six Days of Creation*, vol. 5 of *The Works of Bonaventure: Cardinal, Seraphic Doctor, and Saint*, trans. José de Vinck (Paterson, N.J.: St. Anthony Guild Press, 1970), p. 177.

5. Clare of Assisi, third letter to Agnes of Prague, vv. 12–17 *CA:ED*, p. 51.

Chapter Three: *The Long-Distance Relationship: Loneliness*

1. Mother Teresa of Calcutta, letter to Father Picachy, July 3, 1959, in *Come Be My Light: The Private Writings of the "Saint from Calcutta,"* ed. Brian Kolodiejchuk (New York: Doubleday, 2007), p. 187.

2. Francis of Assisi, "The Office of the Passion," Psalm 6:1–8, in *FA:ED* I, p. 146.

3. Francis of Assisi, "The Office of the Passion," Psalm 6:15–16, in *FA:ED* I, p. 147.

4. Mother Teresa, *Come Be My Light*, pp. 186–187.

5. Mother Teresa, *Come Be My Light*, p. 189.

Chapter Four: *Making a Date With God: Solitude*

1. Francis of Assisi, "A Rule for Hermitages," in *FA:ED* I, p. 61.

Chapter Five: *Becoming an Everyday Mystic: Contemplation*

1. Bonaventure, *On the Six Days of Creation*, p. 94.

2. Ilia Delio, *Franciscan Prayer* (Cincinnati: St. Anthony Messenger Press, 2004), p. 127.

3. Bonaventure, *Itinerarium Mentis in Deum*, 1:7, p. 62.

4. Angela of Foligno, "The *Memorial*: The Stages of Angela's Inner Journey," in *Angela of Foligno: Complete Works*, ed. Paul Lachance (New York: Paulist, 1993), pp. 169–170.

5. Richard McBrien, *Catholicism* (San Francisco: HarperCollins, 1994), p. 1052.

6. Dennis Tamburello, *Ordinary Mysticism* (New York: Paulist, 1996), p. 126.

7. Murray Bodo, *Mystics: Ten Who Show Us the Ways of God* (Cincinnati: St. Anthony Messenger Press, 2007), p. 3.

Chapter Six: *Love Letters From God: The Word*

1. Hugh of St. Victor, *The "Didascalicon" of Hugh of Saint Victor: A Medieval Guide to the Arts,* trans. Jerome Taylor (New York: Columbia University Press, 1991), p. 102.

2. David Lowenherz, ed., *The 50 Greatest Love Letters of All Time* (New York: Random House, 2002), p. xi.

3. Francis of Assisi, "A Letter to the Entire Order," 34–37, in *FA:ED* I, p. 119.

4. Francis of Assisi, "The Later Rule (1223)," 1, in *FA:ED* I, p. 100.

5. Thomas of Celano, "The Life of Saint Francis: The First Book," 9:22, in *FA:ED* I, pp. 201–202.

6. Thomas of Celano, "The Life of Saint Francis: The First Book," 3:7, in *FA:ED* I, p. 188.

7. Richard Rohr and John Feister, *Hope Against Darkness: The Transforming Vision of Saint Francis in an Age of Anxiety* (Cincinnati: St. Anthony Messenger Press, 2001), p. 112.

8. St. Bonaventure, *The Major Legend of Saint Francis,* 11:1, in *FA:ED* II, p. 612.

Chapter Seven: *Being for Others as God Is for Us: Solidarity and Social Justice*

1. Francis of Assisi, "The Testament," v. 14, in *FA:ED* I, p. 125.

2. Francis of Assisi, "Testament," in *FA:ED* I, p. 124.

3. Jacques Dalarun, *Francis of Assisi and Power,* trans. Anne Bartol (St. Bonaventure, N.Y.: Franciscan Institute, 2007), p. 17.

Chapter Eight: *"Praise Be You, Lord, Through Brother Sun": Creation*

1. *FA:ED* I, p. 113.

2. The Assisi Compilation, as cited by Thomas Murtagh in "St. Francis and Ecology," *The Cord* 39 (1989), pp. 99–109.

3. Francis of Assisi, "The Canticle of the Creatures," in *FA:ED* I, pp. 113–114.

4. See Elizabeth Johnson, *Women, Earth, and Creator Spirit* (New York: Paulist, 1993), p. 37.

5. Ilia Delio, Keith Douglass Warner, and Pamela Wood, *Care for Creation: A Franciscan Spirituality of the Earth* (Cincinnati: St. Anthony Messenger Press, 2008), p. 37.

6. Mark Mossa, *Already There: Letting God Find You* (Cincinnati: St. Anthony Messenger Press, 2010), p. 6.

selected bibliography

Angela of Foligno: Complete Works. Edited by Paul Lachance. New York: Paulist, 1993.

Armstrong, Regis, and Ingrid Peterson. *The Franciscan Tradition*. Collegeville, Minn.: Liturgical, 2010.

Bonaventure. *The Works of Bonaventure: Cardinal, Seraphic Doctor, and Saint*. Translated by José de Vinck. Paterson, N.J.: St. Anthony Guild, 1970.

Bodo, Murray. *Landscape of Prayer*. Cincinnati: St. Anthony Messenger Press, 2003.

———. *Mystics: Ten Who Show Us the Ways of God*. Cincinnati: St. Anthony Messenger Press, 2007.

Clare of Assisi: Early Documents. Edited by Regis Armstrong. New York: New City, 2006.

Dalarun, Jacques. *Francis of Assisi and Power*. Translated by Anne Bartol. St. Bonaventure, N.Y.: Franciscan Institute, 2007.

Delio, Ilia. *Franciscan Prayer*. Cincinnati: St. Anthony Messenger Press, 2004.

Delio, Ilia, Keith Douglass Warner, and Pamela Wood. *Care for Creation: A Franciscan Spirituality of the Earth*. Cincinnati: St. Anthony Messenger Press, 2008.

Francis of Assisi: Early Documents. Edited by Regis Armstrong, J.A. Wayne Hellmann, and William Short. 3 volumes. New York: New City, 1999–2001.

Horan, Daniel P. "A Franciscan Approach to Ministry." *Review for Religious* 68 (2009): 132–143.

———. "Dating God: A Young Friar's Experience of Solitude." *America* 196 (2007): 25–27.

————. "Digital Natives and Franciscan Spirituality." *Spiritual Life* 56 (2010): 73–84.

————. "*Koinonia* and the Church in the Digital Age." *Review for Religious* 69 (2010): 230–237.

————. "Praying with the Subtle Doctor: Toward a Contemporary Scotistic Spirituality." *The Cord* 58 (2008): 225–242.

————. "Profit or Prophet? A Franciscan Challenge to Millennials in Higher Education." *AFCU Journal* 8 (2011): 59–73.

————. "St. Francis and the Millennials: Kindred Spirits." *St. Anthony Messenger* 118 (2010): 30–34.

Johnson, Elizabeth. *Women, Earth, and Creator Spirit*. New York: Paulist, 1993.

McBrien, Richard. *Catholicism*. San Francisco: HarperCollins, 1994.

Merton, Thomas. *New Seeds of Contemplation*. New York: New Directions, 1961.

————. *No Man Is an Island*. New York: Harcourt Brace, 1955.

Mossa, Mark. *Already There: Letting God Find You*. Cincinnati: St. Anthony Messenger Press, 2010.

Mother Teresa of Calcutta. *Come Be My Light: The Private Writings of the "Saint from Calcutta."* Edited by Brian Kolodiejchuk. New York: Doubleday, 2007. Murtagh, Thomas. "St. Francis and Ecology." *The Cord* 39 (1989): 99–109.

Rohr, Richard, and John Feister. *Hope Against Darkness: The Transforming Vision of Saint Francis in an Age of Anxiety*. Cincinnati: St. Anthony Messenger Press, 2001.

Tamburello, Dennis. *Ordinary Mysticism*. New York: Paulist, 1996.

ABOUT THE AUTHOR

Daniel P. Horan, O.F.M., a Franciscan friar of Holy Name Province, has published numerous articles on Franciscan spirituality, Thomas Merton, and contemporary systematic theology. He has taught in the department of religious studies at Siena College, led retreats for groups of young adults, and lectured around the United States and in Europe. He currently serves on the board of directors of the International Thomas Merton Society and writes the blog DatingGod.org.

Printed in the United States
By Bookmasters